HER HEART HER HUSTLE

Building a Strategic Relationship Plan for Love & Life

LINDA DENISE WILLIAMS

COPYRIGHT © 2023 BY LINDA DENISE WILLIAMS

The advice and strategies found within may not be suitable for every situation. This work is sold with the understanding that neither the author nor the publisher is held responsible for the results accrued from the advice in this book.

No part of this publication may be reproduced, distributed, or transmitted in any form or by any means, including photocopying, recording, or other electronic or mechanical methods, without the prior written permission of the publisher, except in the case of brief quotations embodied in reviews and certain other non-commercial uses permitted by copyright law.

Printed by:
Self-Publishing Company
Printed in the United States of America
ISBN:979-8-88759-489-7

PREFACE

From the Boardroom to the Bedroom is a guide to create a strategy for a partnership or strengthen an existing relationship. It is formatted and structured just like a business plan. Some of the language is consistent with the language and approach used in writing a business plan. I had to find a way to deliver the information that was succinct, could inspire action and that would deliver a finished product that could be applied to how you manage your relationship. Women who are successful in business have learned how to tap into their masculine energy and thrive in the boardroom with their male counterparts. The structure of the business plan applies to our logical and reasoning mind. What's missing is the switch that nurtures our femininity outside of the boardroom and into the bedroom. Despite the studies and surveys where men say they want a smart, independent career woman on paper, this is not who they marry. Unaware, strong, successful women carry that masculine energy into the relationship where they're authoritative and in charge. They offer to pay, open their own doors, and reach for the check. You can debate me on the facts all you want, but you would be fighting against a man's biology. Men don't care how much money you make, how many degrees you have, what school you went to; if you have not mastered the art and finesse of femininity, a man will walk away because he's not interested in competing with you to do what his biology and programming has designed him to do. Even if you make more money and jump tall buildings in a single bound dressed in a superhero suit with an "S" on your chest, what matters to a man is how you make him feel when he's with you. There's so much to unpack in this journey of self-discovery, but having a strategy, a plan, and clarity about what you want and how to go about getting it is how you start.

ALERT

This process is not up for debate. If you have a better plan, how is that working for you? You know that saying, "Get out of your own way?" *From the Boardroom to the Bedroom* is not the only way to find love; it's "**A**" way. This is not for all women. If what I say resonates with you, then this is for you. This is grown folks' business, straight no chaser. Not everything contained in this blueprint may be an exact match for you. Take the parts that work for you and use them, and the parts that don't, flip the page and keep moving. Do not let one philosophy or perspective deter you from your destination. It is like going to a buffet. You have a variety of food choices, and you get to choose.

This is an investment. Investment implies that there is a seed time and a harvest time. This is a deeply personal yet spiritual journey, and you'll have to slay some demons along the way. I promise you this won't be easy, but you're worth it. You set the pace. Go as fast or as slow as you need to. This is not something you learn one time and you get a certificate to add to your list of accomplishments; this is something that becomes a way of life, a lifestyle that supports your growth and success in every area of your life. As you evolve and transform, so does your business plan.

From the Boardroom to the Bedroom has three components that aid in the deconstruction and design of your relationship plan. 1. Information – you must be informed before you can be transformed. 2. Action – Knowledge is power only when it is applied, and 3. Metrics – You inspect what you respect. This Strategic Relationship Plan is a living, breathing document that should reflect the current condition of your relationship. If you're not reviewing your strategy at least once a month, then less frequently once the relationship has manifested, how do you measure what's working and what's not? In most companies, they're having quarterly meetings to review the financials, the budget, the organization to ensure you're aligned with the vision and mission of the organization. The Executive Team may meet more frequently, but the point of the matter is this: what you give your attention to grows.

Just as a business grows, develops, and expands, so should your relationship. Whether you've never given thought to a relationship intentionally, or you've just been repeating learned behaviors when you're in a relationship, or you're in a relationship and are struggling to decide which way to go, wherever you are on the spectrum, this blueprint is designed to share knowledge and ignite power within you to manifest the partnership you've always wanted but never thought was possible for you to have.

Are you ready? What are you waiting on? Turn the page…

Welcome to the Boardroom,

Linda D. Williams, CVO

Acknowledgments

To the only man who makes me want to be a better woman, Mr. Woodrow Williams. It is his unconditional love that feeds my soul, nourishes my dreams, and increases my capacity to love. I only had the courage to 'jump' because I knew he would not let me fall.

To every sister-friend in my circle, Tamisha Love, Pamela Rogers, Dr. Darnyelle Jervey Harmon, my daughter, Christen M. Dillard, and the countless other women in my tribe, it's your stories, your journey, your unwavering faith, and commitment to my dreams that this project is possible. Thank you.

Table of Contents

Preface 3

Quantum Leap 38

Company Description 65

Market Analysis 81

Marketing Plan 103

Operational Plan 113

Management & Organization 123

Financial Plan 129

The Final Step 153

Executive Summary 153

References 167

About the Author

As a personality, I wear many hats. I have been where many of you are, and if I knew then what I know now, I would have spent more time loving and less time at war with myself and others. I was a mother at 22, a wife by the time I was 23, and divorced twice with three children by the time I was 38. Dating had changed drastically by the time I was reintroduced to the open market, and I was ill-equipped to play the game. I couldn't tell you what I wanted but I could write chapter and verse about what I didn't want. I was not clear and aligned with what I really wanted in a partner and what I really wanted in a relationship beyond not wanting a liar and a cheater, so I got a hodgepodge of individuals showing up, each having something I wanted but often falling short of what I needed. Dating just felt like I was always giving more than I was getting. After being in a relationship for 19 years, I was conditioned to giving more than I was getting in return, sacrificing self for the benefit of others, putting myself last, and bartering my emotional and mental currency to maintain an image of a successful power couple, and oh yeah, we were supposed to be happy.

Are you a successful, intelligent, financially stable, got-it-going-on boss struggling to find someone who complements your swag, elevates your style of play, and causes you to want to be a better woman? #ThatUsedToBeMe. Perhaps you're in a relationship, feeling unfulfilled, wondering what's the point of it all, not sure if you should stay and fight or throw in the towel and cut your losses; hell, life is meant to be enjoyed, savored, marinated and you deserve to be happy. For two decades after my divorce, I found myself with guys whose resume made them the ideal candidate for the position until they got the job then their representative retired and the real Slim Shady emerged. I finally made peace at the age of 50 with the fact that being single for the rest of my life and having a seasonal worker from time to time or an STD (**S**omething **T**o **D**o) may be my lot in life, and I was okay with it or so I thought; yet subconsciously, I still looked at the ring finger of every man who caught my attention, his swag, his hair, his teeth, his shoes, and wondered if he were emotionally and physically available. In my imagination I narrated a story that would end up with him needing my money, my credit, my emotional currency, or my talents to elevate him in some way. That was my defense mechanism kicking in so I wouldn't have to go through the bullshit. Funny, as I write these words, I'm sure there is a man somewhere saying the same thing about us. But that's what happens when you do community service. You're in the business of giving, not receiving. I wasn't desperate for a relationship, I was deserving of a partnership, and the path I was on was a lonely, unfulfilled highway to more of the same.

If you're reading this book, there's something in my story that resonates with you. I'm a living witness that I found the love of my life at 53 because that was my true heart's desire. I'm not ashamed to admit that I am better in a partnership than I am as a Lone Ranger. Hope is a feeling of expectation and desire for a certain thing to happen. Used as a verb, it means "to expect with confidence" or "to cherish a desire with anticipation." If you live long enough, you'll have some battle scars and may still be carrying some baggage, some limiting beliefs that are getting in the way of the love you want. If you're willing to change your thoughts, you can change your life. The biggest threat to the love you want is the story you keep telling yourself and the narrator is what I call "The Roommate." A 'Roommate" is a person occupying the same room as another. In this context, the "Roommate" is the voice in your head. From the time you wake up in the morning until the time you go to bed, this voice is talking nonstop all day, every day. Have you ever paid attention? Its constant chatter is about nothing, and the rest is all commentary. I bet you thought this nonstop conversation that's taking place in your head was you, didn't you? How is that possible? If you can recognize, acknowledge, and hear the voice, then how can you be the voice? And unaware, we get sucked into the constant banter of incessant talking as if this voice were speaking wisdom into a situation, or even worse, has a solution to the problem. The voice has a strong egoic influence that often betrays us in our time of need.

I took the path less traveled because there is an elite group of women who are successful in business, in their careers, but have failed to find success in their personal relationships. The challenge you encounter is how to create harmony between the masculine energy that serves you well in business but often destroys your love life, and the feminine energy needed to thrive in a relationship that may threaten your career or business. My objective is to provide a solution by leveraging a tool used in business called a business plan to create a strategy, a roadmap to how you approach and manifest harmony and cultivate growth in your intimate relationship.

Think of this Strategic Relationship Plan as a blueprint to build the foundation, and the tools and techniques shared are the raw materials needed to construct your forever home, your partnership. Practice the pearls and principles you learn in this book, implement the techniques and strategies outlined in this blueprint, not just to attract your life partner or improve your relationship but also to improve your finances, career, and health. Ralph Waldo Emerson said, "The mind, once stretched by a new idea, never returns to its original dimensions."

Thank you for allowing me to accompany you on this life-changing journey to releasing the full expression of who you are and the powerful impact you'll make in the lives of others.

Introduction to the CEO

What is a CEO? CEO stands for Chief Executive Officer who is the highest-ranking executive of a firm. CEOs act as the company's public face and make major corporate decisions. In 2009, I was laid off from a Fortune 500 company and had decided to turn my speaking and coaching experience into a business. I received a grant and decided to take a class at the University of Delaware on How to Write a Business Plan. This was a 10-week course that at the end of the class would produce a Business Plan that could be taken to a bank or given to an Angel Investor to raise capital to fund the business. I've always been passionate about the psychology of relationships and have worked with individuals and couples over the years counseling and coaching them through the cycles of life that many couples encounter throughout different phases in their relationships. One day, I awoke, wondering if women managed their relationships the way they manage their business, would they be more successful in their intimate partnerships? This epiphany has led me to my life's work: *From the Boardroom to the Bedroom: Her Heart. Her Hustle… Building a Strategic Relationship Plan for Love & Life*.

I remember my first boyfriend was when I was in third grade, Jesse Simmons. He used to bring me penny candy, Now & Later, Lincoln Logs, Sweet Tarts, and bubble gum every day as he walked me to class. Ahhhh, Chivalry. Creating expectations of what a man should do; to provide and protect at the age of 8.

Are you a woman who loves hard, gives a thousand percent in a relationship? Do you often feel empty because your needs go unmet? Do you tell him what you want, but he gives you what he thinks you should be satisfied with? Are you over the whole dating scene or running on fumes in your current relationship? People always talk about giving back, but how much more community service (defined as voluntary work intended to help people in a particular area) are you going to give before you have paid your debt to society.

This is the landscape that most individuals feel helpless to navigate their way through when trying to achieve a healthy, loving, supportive, authentic relationship. And the truth is you can't get to intimacy without going through vulnerability. Vulnerability = self-love. Vulnerability = forgiveness. Vulnerability = acceptance. Vulnerability = transparency. Vulnerability lives in the light, not the darkness. Vulnerability = The capacity to Love and be loved.

If you are in a relationship, are you out of balance? Are you juggling work and romance? If you have children, is self-care the last item on the checklist of things to do or did it not make the list at all? Do you have obligations outside the home that compete or add to existing responsibilities, and, somehow, you're still expected to be a lady in the streets and a freak under the sheets? The Strategic Relationship Plan is a tool to create crystal clear clarity and direction in how to navigate through or around the roadblocks that are getting in the way of joy and harmony in a relationship. When you make an appointment to see a doctor for something other than a routine check-up, it's because you have physical symptoms that an over-the-counter remedy cannot fix. Before the doctor prescribes something stronger than what you've been taking, they first must look at your medical history, a list of current medications, review family history, and find out what prompted you to seek professional help in the first place. They then perform an exam to see if they can diagnose the problem through observation or need to take some samples and have them sent to the lab for further testing. Finding the love you want and keeping the love you have is a process. Love is a seed that when planted into good ground, attended to, nourished, and pruned, can grow, prosper, and bear fruit.

I have found that in a microwave society, many people are looking for a genie that can grant them three wishes and solve all their problems. Anything worth having requires some level of investment in time, money, and resources. You'll have to take off the mask, you'll have to remove the wall that you've built around your pain, and you'll need support. One of the biggest enemy's to healing and restoration is the shame that protects the secrets. The light that destroys the darkness is the salve for healing, and the anointing of peace. You cannot attract a healthy, loving, nourishing relationship if you carry the wounds of your past into your future. Instead of building a wall around the pain to prevent anything from rubbing up against it, causing you to be reinjured, why not remove the thorn so the wound can heal and then there's no wall to build or barriers to overcome?

Through this process, you'll define what you want, identify areas of improvement that are worth investing in to make the relationship better, and confront what you've known all along and didn't have the courage to acknowledge. Not all businesses are successful. Part of a business plan is to have an exit strategy in the event things don't go as planned. Having an exit strategy is not a self-fulfilling prediction or a lack of faith that causes your relationship to fail. If anything, it will take the pressure off trying to force a round peg into a square hole. Having options creates freedom. Unfortunately, on average, the length of a marriage in the U.S. is seven to eight years. Some states have a higher rate than others, but the divorce rate for the country is around fifty percent.

What I learned in How to Write a Business Plan class has become the blueprint for creating a strategy and a plan for a healthy, thriving relationship. We make plans all the time. We make plans for vacation, the holidays, dinner; yet how many people plan their relationship? Armagno (2016) reported that students in the graduating class of 1979 from the Harvard MBA Business School were asked a single question about their goals in life in a research study on goal setting. The question was this:

Have you set written goals and created a plan for their attainment?

Prior to graduation, it was determined that:
- 84% of the entire class had set no goals at all

- 13% of the class had set written goals but had no concrete plans
- 3% of the class had both written goals and concrete plans

The results?

Well, you have likely somewhat guessed it. Ten years later, the 13% of the class that had set written goals but had not created plans, were making twice as much money as the 84% of the class that had set no goals at all.

However, the apparent kicker is that the 3% of the class that had both written goals and a plan, were making ten times as much as the rest of the 97% of the class.

Ten times as much, insane! Are intimate relationships more personal than a business? Absolutely, and the same logic women tend to use to manage successful businesses does not always translate to how they manage their relationships because emotion often trumps logic. We are intentional about our careers, health, and money, but what about our intimate partnerships? The Boardroom is where we'll lay the foundational principles to understand how the mind works. This is critical to how you'll create the partner and relationship you want. This is where you obtain the knowledge of how the game is played, and the Bedroom is where you use your most powerful assets, your imagination to bring about manifestation – the physical result of what you have created.

A threat to the success of building a partnership is learning how to manage the power of your emotions. Your emotions are a critical part of your Guidance System, sort of like an internal GPS. You program the destination of where you want to go and trust your Guidance System to have access to the best route to get you there. Knowing what lies ahead, your Guidance System can warn you by sending an alert, a red flag that's always felt in your body, it may reroute you or inform you of delays ahead, as well as give reassurance that you're still on the fastest route to your destination.

From The Boardroom to the Bedroom is the process of transformation one must go through to deprogram ingrained beliefs that no longer serve you. Or maybe you're struggling to find that harmony of partnership and expansion and growth of self. If you're a woman who wants to be in a committed relationship and/or married, welcome to the Boardroom. The CEO is a mind-altering drug. Will you acknowledge that if you knew how to have a healthy, fulfilling, and committed relationship you would not be reading this book? If you knew what to do differently to have better communication, be understood, and be fulfilled in the relationship without having to give up anything, you wouldn't need this book. Many of you are fractured and you have just learned to live with the aches and pains you think are normal in relationships. "Your Roommate" has convinced you that this is the price of admission. Why are you successful in business but not in love? What are three characteristics you would say make you a great businessperson? Do you find those same personality traits manifest in your relationships? What has been the feedback from others? Have you drawn a line in the sand and are unwilling to compromise, to meet each other halfway?

I found unconditional love when I learned what I'll teach you in the Boardroom. Learning the Universal Laws and Principles have been a game changer and the secret to having a healthy, loving and committed relationship. You'll learn these teachings throughout the development of your Strategic Relationship Plan whether you're in a relationship now or you want to be in one.

COME…. Walk with me…before we assemble in the Boardroom, let's observe the transformation of an Imago…

As a Relationship Strategist, I'll use my expertise to guide you through what's analogous to the metamorphosis of a caterpillar becoming a butterfly. **NOTHING CHANGES UNTIL YOU CHANGE!** Observe the lifecycle of becoming:

Chrysalis

Coming out of a tiny egg, the caterpillar spends its time eating. [When you're in the Boardroom, this is where you'll consume the fundamental principles that will equip you with the tools you'll need as you go through the transformation process]. Once satisfied, she prepares for her incredible metamorphosis to become an imago, a butterfly. Caterpillars weave a silk cocoon, in which they will become a chrysalis, the intermediate stage between the caterpillar and the butterfly. As the CEO, you'll begin to internalize the knowledge and apply the teachings that will transform your mind, how you approach your life, your relationships.

Metamorphosis

The Caterpillar Digests Itself

In the chrysalis, it is a real upheaval. In one to two weeks, the caterpillar's organs evolve, giving birth to the nymph, the future butterfly. The brain and eyes enlarge, the antennae lengthen, the mandibles shrink, and the proboscis appears. A proboscis is a tubular sucking organ, the proboscis enables a butterfly to extract sweet nectar from the flowers it feeds upon, regardless of the shape of the blossom.

Inside the chrysalis, the caterpillar will digest itself; its whole body is dissolved by enzymes and reduced to a semi-liquid state. As you immerse yourself in the knowledge available in the Boardroom, it will destroy your old beliefs and create new beliefs, a new way of thinking, a more confident and clearer path to where you're going. As you continue to evolve, you'll reach higher heights and go to deeper depths to experience places you heard about but now are experiencing.

Left intact are the imaginal discs made up of stem cells, which will absorb proteins from the remains of the caterpillar and create a whole new body. Your core values will remain intact and are the building blocks for how you operate in relationships.

The length of the process varies depending on the species, but after about two weeks, the butterfly emerges from its chrysalis.

Only you can determine how long it will take. Unforgiveness of self and others lengthens the process. Not letting go of the pain, blaming others, even if justified, lengthens the process. Everything has an energy, a vibration. What you focus on, give your attention to is what's attracted to you. We live in the physical realm where there's the buffer of time. Not everything you think or do has immediate consequences. Hermes Trismegistus said, "As above, so below, as within, so without." "As within" presumes what we think deep within ourselves, how well we know ourselves. "So without" supposes that it will get expressed in the life we lead, what we manifest.

For the caterpillar to transform into a butterfly, it undergoes an anatomical change (transformation in its shape and body structure) called metamorphosis. The process begins when the insect becomes a pupa, a period in which it doesn't move and remains within a kind of protection. For some of you, as scary as it may seem, you're going to have to sit still. Learn to say "NO." I know you don't like it… I know it's uncomfortable… "Alone" is defined as separate, apart, or isolated from others. "Lonely" is defined as destitute of sympathetic or friendly companionship, interacting through talk or sex, support, etc. For those of you in relationships, how many times has your significant other been in the same room and yet you were lonely? Physically, they're there, but there's no attention, interaction, affection, conversation, etc.

How long is this going to take? The butterfly will finally see the light of day when the external conditions (sun, humidity) are favorable. This can take up to several months for some species. During this time, the nymph lives on the food reserves made by the caterpillar. You'll gauge progress by the feedback you receive from the Universe. What you're experiencing and responding to in the physical world is how you recognize the change.

Emergence

The emergence is when the imago finally breaks its chrysalis to prepare to take off. It swells its abdomen more and more and, little by little, cracks the chrysalis from which it's released in a few minutes. It begins by sticking out the head, the legs, and, lastly, the wings.

All crumpled up, she then needs a few hours of respite, wings down, to finish getting ready. When the butterfly's wings are very rigid and dry, it can finally take flight. It forages the nectar of wildflowers to feed and looks for a partner to reproduce.

Anytime you want to go to the next level in your career, body, finances, or relationship, you must shed your old way of thinking and level up. Acquire new skills, embrace a different way of thinking, and shift the way you move in the world because to get to the next level, you're going to have to do some things you've never done before.

This manual is designed to take a deep dive into the business of you. Being in a healthy relationship requires you to know who you are and what you want. When you "go public," what you attract is an indicator of who you are. If you are in an existing relationship and things are not as you hoped they would be, going through this process will help you identify areas of opportunity to reassess your plan and determine if you need to renegotiate the terms of your contract or if dissolution of that merger is something to consider. Nevertheless, similar to the butterfly, the struggle to break out of the chrysalis is necessary to build strength so you can fly.

You may find you need a little more time. Areas that are still under construction need repair and, therefore, it's not prudent to go public just yet or to schedule a board meeting until you're ready to present your findings to the other shareholders and have some solutions for the opportunities identified. Whatever the outcome, the process will be invaluable. It will identify gaps in some areas of your portfolio and reveal things that you may not have been aware of in a unique way.

Being empowered is the gift I want to give to every woman who goes through this process. This blueprint is not meant to be done in a day, but it's designed to challenge some deep-rooted beliefs that we have acquired in the last 50 years with the feminist movement as well as cultural beliefs and even unconscious programming we're recycling that are damaging our ability to have authentic, unconditional loving relationships.

This is an unorthodox strategy to finding the love you want or keeping and strengthening the love you have. In some situations, it may be like ripping the band aid off a wound so it can get some air. Then you can assess if staying is more detrimental than walking away. When you evaluate stock, you look at how it has performed over the years, and, sometimes, past behavior is a predictor of future success. And it will be up to you to decide whether or not to continue investing in a stock that's on a downward trend and has been losing money for years, and decide to cut your losses. OR is there something unique about this opportunity that's worth fighting for? Maybe it's seeking help outside the relationship that changes the game. Those decisions and choices will be up to you, the CEO of your company. Armed with a clear vision and purpose of where you want the company to be will provide the anchor you need to sell your shares or reinvest in the company. This book is not here to debate political, cultural, and socioeconomic issues or isms that exist in the world today. My objective is to guide women into their own personal power and divine intuition to live the love they dream about.

Disclaimer

Utilizing this framework provides the proven strategies that have helped thousands upon thousands of individuals find the love that they seek in a relationship, significantly improve the quality of the relationship that they're in, or bring clarity to create an exit strategy to dissolve a partnership that no longer serves them.

This is a blueprint template designed for anyone who wants to be in a committed relationship. The company you're building is the business of YOU. Before you go public and expose yourself to other companies that are looking to merge and create a partnership, you want to make sure you're fully equipped with the tools and resources to be successful.

If you're in an existing relationship and want to level up in certain areas, the process will help you to identify the gaps and offer strategies to improve in those areas. If you decide, after developing a relationship strategy, that you've mismanaged your company, or your existing partner is no longer a good fit for where the company is going, then it may be prudent to seek outside counsel on the best way to move forward to dissolve the merger and rebuild elsewhere.

From the Boardroom to the Bedroom is not designed to offer legal or professional counsel on your situation. It is merely a tool to provide you with the knowledge and power to change your thoughts, to deconstruct limiting beliefs that are sabotaging your relationships. When you change your thoughts, you change your life.

James Allen said that we don't attract that which we want but that which we are. If you don't do the work from the inside out, you can make lists all day long of what you want in a partner, but what you'll attract will be a manifestation of who you are.

Not all sections will apply to the business of you.

I prefer you do the work to process your thoughts and create strategies in a *Journal*; however, I recognize some of you cannot read your own handwriting so typing your answers in a *Digital Journal* will provide an alternative avenue to do the work in written form as you develop your Strategic Relationship Plan. This book will always serve as the original template so as you create a strategy for the relationship after the merger, it will continue to be a North Star, a reminder of the purpose and intention of why you exist in the first place, and you can always begin again if needed.

How to Navigate Through the Book

A lot of information acquired from multiple sources over the years that have impacted my life is contained in these pages. The recommendation to use a *Journal* gives you the space to process your thoughts and emotions as you work your way through each chapter and provide a place to practice what you are learning in the Boardroom. The exercises are designed to identify gaps in your existing process that may be getting in the way of you receiving your Ideal Mate or thrive in the relationship that you want. What limiting beliefs or belief systems are disguised as truths that you've been holding on to?

I recently had a conversation with my 35-year-old daughter. Organically, we were talking about how much she has grown and how her perspective has evolved in relationships. She began to share a memory of when she was a teenager, with her room being right next to our bedroom, she overheard a very heated and violent argument. As a child, she hated her father because he was an asshole, and she did not like me so much because she did not know why I stayed in a relationship that dishonored me. She thought I deserved so much better. That day, the argument got so heated, and she was so scared that he might be hurting me that she burst through the door, not knowing what she would find. Would I be in a pool of blood with him attacking and hurting me? As you could probably imagine, not knowing what was going on the other side of that bedroom door, the fear and anxiety she felt in her imagination in that moment and many others before just like it created trauma. Trauma is **the lasting emotional response that often results from living through a distressing event**. Experiencing a traumatic event can harm a person's sense of safety, sense of self, and ability to regulate emotions and navigate relationships. This is a trauma she has carried all these years. Of course, I had no idea of the trauma the ongoing arguments would have on her, since these were not things we talked about. We would just act like nothing happened and go on about our business. 20 years later, every time she remembered that experience, she was transported back to that 15-year-old helpless teenager who lived in fear that every argument might be the one argument that got out of control. For 20 years, she has carried that memory and it has affected her relationships unknowingly. She would say "I'm over it, I'm past it, I've let it go. So, I don't know why I still get emotional when I talk about it." With unconditional love and empathy, I was able to provide much needed insight into that day, about her father, about why he was the way he was toward women that helped her confront the fear she carried. She has since been able to heal that childhood trauma that affected her up until that conversation. What are you carrying in your subconscious, the storehouse of your memories, that you're unaware of that may be silently affecting your choice in men? What triggers take you from 0 to 60 in 10 seconds? What words cause you to immediately become defensive, make you want to punch somebody in the face or worse, withdraw, shut down, and go mute? I share this with you to simply say, not everything is obvious. We don't often know why we're the way we are or why we act and react the way we do in certain situations. I hope that you accept this challenge to uncover and heal those hidden strongholds that are affecting your ability to have a partnership and thrive in it.

The Law of Attraction says you can only attract what you are, so if what you want is not what you're getting, then it's time to look at the source. The exercises are the fertilizers to the seeds you're sowing with the knowledge you're being exposed to. Every time you focus and give attention to your relationship plan it's like water and sunlight needed to help the seed to thrive.

In the beginning, you may ask how these questions will help you find your mate. If you attract what you are, and you don't have the kind of person you feel you deserve, then, like a physician, you must first run some tests to see if you can figure out what's going on in the body. In the Strategic Relationship Plan, you deal with the mind. You must uncover your limiting beliefs that are creating roadblocks to partnership. You must work through every area of the company to ensure you're aligned to what you say you want. At the end of this process, you may find your relationship plan is solid. If this is true, but you're still single and experiencing low-quality options, then one of two things may be the culprit. 1. You plant the seed with your intentions, but you turn around and pull it out of the ground with your words of doubt and unbelief. 2. You don't have clear boundaries of what you're unwilling to accept. You give chances that are not deserved or earned. You accept or allow what you don't want in hopes that he'll change and give you what you need. Every second that someone takes up your time with little to no benefit to you is one second longer to the not allowing of your Ideal Mate, the partnership that you really want.

You must be willing to identify those who align with you, your goals, your core values, and where you're going. If they don't, say "Thank You" and let them go. There are also missed opportunities when you're the culprit. Remember, the Universe is always giving you feedback. When you start trying to control by demanding actions to be performed by others as if they were circus animals, this won't end well for you. Your fear is causing the controlling behavior. Stop it! Check your internal conversation. What story are you telling yourself? You are creating the roadblocks and blaming the other person for not going around your self-induced roadblocks to prove they're worthy of you. Stop it!

One of the strategies to relationship building is understanding the collaboration between the conscious and subconscious mind to create what you call your reality. Nothing happens by accident, but something can happen out of the oblivious, out of you not paying attention or not being aware of what's happening in you. All lives matter, but all lives are not equal; have you not noticed? If you fail to understand the powerful relationship between the conscious and subconscious mind and its ability to create your reality, then you'll fall into a life of conformity, being like everybody else. The greatest threat to courage is conformity. The 5% who have it figured out continue to live life despite a recession, inflation, fluctuations in the stock market, or whatever political party is in control of the House and the Senate, while others experience the rollercoaster ride of life in quiet desperation.

The blueprint within these pages has not only the keys to create an amazing relationship but also the keys to the kingdom you call your reality. James Allen, in *"As a Man Thinketh,"* wrote, "As he thinks, so he is; as he continues to think, so he remains."

Enlightenment starts with awareness. I invite you to come on this incredible and life-changing journey. Let's create the relationship you want, not the relationship you settle for. You can do this. I have spent hundreds of thousands of dollars on countless programs from wealth building opportunities, improved health programs, quick weight loss programs, all kinds of pills and powders, books, classes, and certifications, looking for an easy solution. In full transparency, I didn't get the results I expected. Why? I didn't do the work. I wanted to take a pill and eat whatever I wanted with no exercise and be thin or read a book on what wealthy people do and be a multimillionaire in 90 days. Maybe those things work for other people, but **NOTHING CHANGED UNTIL I CHANGED**. I wish I could tell you that I started loving myself and that was my motivation to change. I got sick and tired of being sick and tired. It should have been enough, but it wasn't. The catalyst for me to keep my commitments to myself was my husband. After I created a relationship strategy, what keeps me locked in is wanting to live the rest of my life laughing and loving, enjoying every second I have left with my husband. I can only speak for myself, but I am better in a partnership than I am by myself. My purpose is to be fulfilled with him, using my gifts and talents to serve the world and create immense wealth. Every other relationship I had was mere growth and development (G&D). It may not be that for you. If you haven't given up and can stand in your truth and confess that you want to share this life with someone, regardless of the success you have amassed, then I invite you to design your Strategic Relationship Plan.

NOTHING CHANGES UNTIL YOU CHANGE!

If you are reading this book, then you've earned the right to know my story. I live the love I teach in this book every day, and it's possible for you too. There's no lack because the secret of unconditional love is not needing him to change to make me happy. Take responsibility for your own happiness; there's no hole that can ever be filled outside of yourself. That means his job is not to validate you, affirm you, motivate you, etc. Why not? Anything that is a need you must seek outside of yourself makes you a puppet. It makes you dependent. What happens when that person, that drug, that comfort food isn't there to make you feel better? You move into desperation. You overreact, blow things out of proportion, and start becoming demanding, aggressive, over-the-top. How long does a person last carrying the responsibility of your emotional dysfunction all because you will not take responsibility for your pain? I'm not saying the other person should abandon you, but, in my experience, the other person can never do enough to satisfy that bottomless hole in your heart. People are fickle and undisciplined emotions are dangerous.

Partnership implies agreement. Partnership implies alignment. Partnership demands maturity. How can two walk together unless they agree. Agreement on your core values is essential. If you want children and he doesn't, is it reasonable to hope that one day he will change his mind? Maybe he will. Maybe he hasn't met a woman like you. But how long are you willing to wait? A woman's peak reproductive years are between the late teens and late 20s. **By age 30**, fertility (the ability to get pregnant) starts to decline. This decline becomes more rapid once you reach your mid-30s. By 45, fertility has declined so much that getting pregnant naturally is unlikely for most women. **OR** is the path of least resistance to be with someone who also wants children? If they make it clear they are not ready to commit and don't know when they will be, you're resentful because you're 2 years in and the marriage conversation isn't even a conversation. Decide. Stay or go but be happy with whatever decision you make. It is not his fault your wifey material and he doesn't want to put a ring on it. Bounce. It is your fault if you stay with unrealistic expectations. Are there exceptions where people were together for 8 years and finally the guy proposed? Yes, but that is not the majority. All I'm saying is, don't stay and complain and be unhappy when you can leave and find someone who wants what you want. The Strategic Relationship Plan is designed to create clarity. Once you know what you want, then you must create action, execute the plan. As you're implementing and executing the plan, you must have accountability, whether that's through one-on-one coaching, seminars, attendance at live events, participating in group session calls, or friend to friend(s). This is a sisterhood that we're forging to undergird one another through shared experiences and life lessons. I believe in you, and I believe that the partnership you create will be a gift to serve your legacy and the world.

Now that you've created a solid foundation upon which to build a strategy, set aside a certain amount of time each day to attend to the development and execution of your plan. The Strategic Relationship Plan will be your roadmap to how you navigate dating, improve an existing relationship, or come to terms with the dissolution of an existing relationship.

May your life be filled with endless love, prosperity, and health to infinity and beyond.

STATEMENT OF WORK

The knowledge contained within these pages are to provide a roadmap, a guide, to the love you want, not the love you have settled for. Searching the web provides countless ways to find your life partner along with several sites that provide a smorgasbord of options to what you think "The One" looks like with a well-crafted profile and some head shots or revealing photos of their assets to entice you to subscribe to find out more. Some have personality, chemistry, or compatibility tests to improve your odds of finding "The One." Although well intended and there may be some value in those tests, despite your best efforts, your love life feels like a dog chasing its tail. How do you know what is real? Are people who they say they are?

Maybe you were like me, I had a successful career, I traveled extensively so it was hard to meet emotionally and physically available men that were secure with my lifestyle and to whom I was attracted. The men I encountered were either married, fat, gay, immature, insecure, or just not interested in or ready for commitment. Long distance wasn't an option, wanting a child or having small children was not an option, insecure, needy, low self-esteem-- unattractive, commitment phobia, self-absorbed, and on and on, the list of not interested continued to grow. It grew so long that I finally gave up on ever finding a mate because I had too much shit with me and somehow being alone was better than lowering my standards.

Just Breathe

Before an architect begins to build, there's something called a Pre-Design phase. This is where they learn everything possible about their clients' personality, lifestyle, and needs as well as try to better understand how much space they need now and likely to need in the future, and how the space should be used, organized, and arranged. As the architect of your relationship, there must be a shift in your mindset; otherwise, you'll continue to do what you've always done, the familiar, what's comfortable. It's critical that you digest the principles described to you in their entirety. Like the caterpillar, it spends most of its time eating, including the leaf it was born on. In fact, caterpillars can be quite picky when it comes to what leaf to eat, which is why the principles taught in building the foundation in your relationship plan are vital for you to learn. Failure to practice these truths consistently may lead to incomplete metamorphosis.

As we prepare to embark on this journey, we need a space to create. When you're ready to get started, find a place where you're least likely to be interrupted. Set the timer if you like to commit to whatever time you have available to invest in yourself each day. Do this every day until you have completed your Strategic Relationship Plan. Then, at least once a week, until your relationship has physically manifested, review and update as needed. Remember, we inspect what we respect. Check-in weekly to make sure you have followed through on your action items and update as needed. After you are physically enjoying your partnership, I would share this (if you have not already done so) with your partner and set out to create a strategy for the merged company to create a plan for how the two of you will move in the world as one. Once completed, this should be viewed and updated at least on a quarterly basis moving forward.

If you're ready, like the caterpillar, I want to escort you inside the Chrysalis. Here's where we lay the foundation for transformation. I'll take you inside how the mind works. Unveil Universal Principles necessary to bring about transformation. Read this section repeatedly until it becomes ingrained into every cell of your being. Wisdom is the principal thing; therefore, get wisdom: and with all thy getting, get understanding. What's wisdom? Wisdom is the quality of having experience, knowledge, and good judgment.

In the next few pages, we will move into a stage that may be overwhelming at first. Information I didn't create, but I did manifest it. When I asked the right questions, these were the answers that showed up. I take no credit for being the originator of this knowledge, but none of what we're learning is new because there's nothing new under the sun. The way it's being revealed to each of us is new to us, but this information has existed always. I am just the messenger; I said, send me, I'll go.

To your success,

QUANTUM LEAP

An abrupt change, inspiration, breakthrough, a physical event.

How The Mind Works

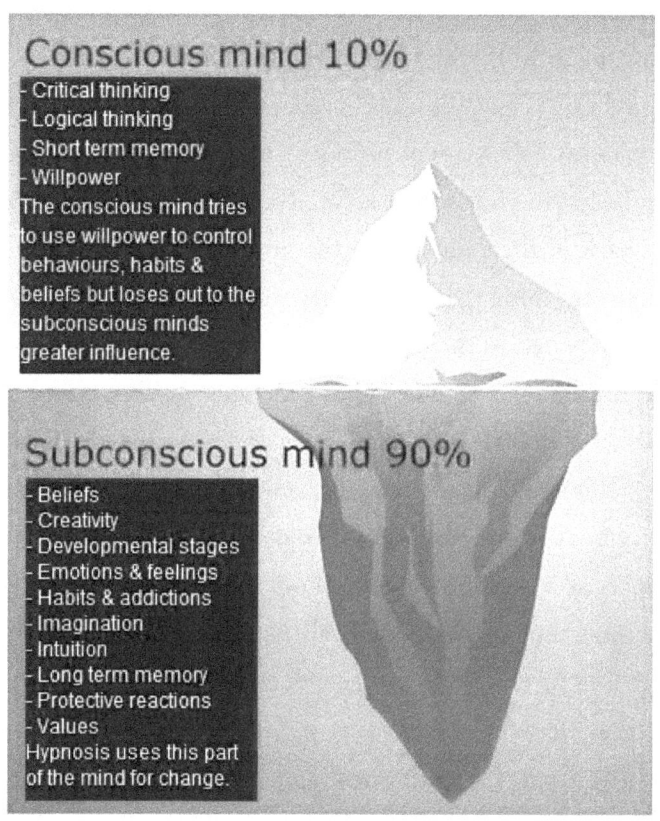

We have one mind divided into two spheres. You have your conscious mind which is logical and rational. Throughout life, we experience two sides; objective and subjective, visible, and invisible, thought and its manifestation. How does this partnership work? When we have a thought, it is received by our conscious reasoning mind. Do you ever have a thought that you think about so much that it creates a reaction, and you feel it in your stomach? Abraham Hicks says that if you think on a thought for 16 seconds another thought like it will be attracted to it. Keep attention on that thought for another 16 seconds. Another thought will be attracted to it. If you continue to hold your attention to that thought (16, 32, 48, 64, 80....), you will have created such momentum that it will produce an emotion. That emotion can be felt in your solar plexus. The solar plexus is located at the back of the stomach, or the upper abdomen. The attention to anything that creates an emotion is where the impression is created in the subconscious mind.

Your subconscious mind operates automatically and quickly with little or no effort and no sense of voluntary control. This allows us to perceive the world around us, recognize objects, orientate attention, avoid losses, and fear potential threats. It is also the domain of our emotions, the storehouse for our memories and our values. The subconscious mind will use our emotions, past experiences and learning to help us intuitively make decisions.

Why is any of this information important? Whenever we have a problem, it is natural for us to approach the problem just using our conscious mind – logic and reason. For example, getting fit, you create a SMART goal around going to the gym three times a week, you buy your workout gear and equipment, and you sign up for classes. You set yourself a goal and break those goals into small, bite-sized pieces to create a plan. You're excited and you tell people about your goal and this time you even consider getting a personal trainer or workout buddy to support you and hold you accountable. You watch videos and take advice from experienced people. Would you agree that this is a recipe for success? You then consciously use your willpower to push yourself to your goal and spend every effort to make your new activity a habit.

You'll probably give up after a while, or even if you're successful, it will feel like a struggle. It is so hard. Why? Go back to the diagram of the two minds above. Which part does all the activity fall into? All your efforts are slow, deliberate, and require conscious thought and focus. You're using that part of the brain with limited bandwidth with some success, but it's exhausting.

Look at the diagram again and consider,
- What part of our minds are responsible for habits?
- Which creates the impulse to pursue the goal in the first place?
- Which part is quick and effortless?

We need to use both parts but knowing which one to use at the right time is key.

Conclusion

This is how thoughts turn to things. You have a thought; *I want to lose weight.* Instead of thinking about how hard it is to lose weight, think about what you'll look like and how much more energy you'll have and how good you'll feel in that little black dress. Imagining that experience with such clarity impresses it on your subconscious. Your subconscious, which is the seat of your emotions and the storehouse of your memories, generates suggestions for the conscious mind based on impressions, intuitions, intentions, and feelings. If you're struggling to move forward with something, the answer lies in these areas. The strategy to change behavior and your limiting beliefs is in finding a way to feel what you want so that when you have a conscious thought, it aligns with what you believe and then it's made manifest.

Faith is the evidence of something that's not seen; the confidence, the belief, the trust that it's so even though there's no physical proof. When you think and believe in something in the absence of any evidence that it's true, thoughts turn to things. And the time between thought and manifestation is the distance between what you say you want and what you believe you can have.

Let's go a little bit deeper with understanding how to live in our future now and explore one of the most powerful principles in the Universe, the Law of Assumption.

The Law of Assumption

Law of Assumption

The Law of Assumption, championed by Neville Lancelot Goddard, an American philosopher, takes the reverse approach. It states that if we act and feel as if our goals and aspirations have already happened, they will manifest. The law of assumption proposes that what we assume to be true will come true. You always go to the end, and the end is where you begin.

Stephen Covey said, "To begin with the end in mind means to start with a clear understanding of your destination. It means to know where you're going so that you better understand where you are now so that the steps you take are always in the right direction."

When I was a Road Warrior, I figured out how to travel well. Wherever I was going, I would always look at the forecast for the time I would be in that city. Living in Atlanta, the weather was mild compared to the winters in other states. If the temperature was 75 or 80 degrees in Atlanta, but 40 degrees in Michigan, I would dress for where I was and pack for where I was going. I knew that the plane is always cold, so I would carry a shawl in my carry on. When I landed, I would go to the bathroom and take out my jacket, scarf, and gloves if needed before I went to get the rental car. This illustrates that you can be content where you are while you're preparing for where you're going. I knew I was going to Michigan. I knew it was going to be cold the whole week. Preparation before I arrived set me up for continued success. This is the mindset mastery we're looking to achieve with an understanding of the Universal Laws. Exhibit behaviors now of where you're going regardless of where you are.

The reason operating in the principle of the Law of Assumption is that we struggle because we're at war with our conscious mind. To get to a place where you can imagine, visualize, dream of being the person you want to become, or experience the love you desire happens first in your imagination, and the first indication of manifestation is the feeling evoked from imagining having that experience right now. The subconscious mind cannot differentiate between what you call real (the physical experience) from what you imagine.

Meditation is a vehicle that can transport people mentally out of their reality where decisions need to be made, problems need to be solved, strategies created into a deep sleep or the 4th stage of sleep, REM sleep, and awake, rested, and energized. Insomnia can be a result of an undisciplined mind that disrupts deep or REM sleep. Too many studies have demonstrated the need for sleep to function optimally.

Intentionality or mindfulness has a measurable impact on certain brain chemicals. Serotonin increases; this "feel good" chemical helps regulate mood. Cortisol, the stress hormone, decreases. DHEA levels are boosted, increasing longevity, and improving mood, fatigue, and well-being. In one study, women who took DHEA supplements reported improved sexuality and sense of well-being, including fewer feelings of depression and anxiety. These are some of the many benefits to meditation.

Mind and Matter

Mind is the master power that molds and makes,
And we are Mind, and evermore we take,
The tool of thought, and shaping what we will,
Bring forth a thousand joys, a thousand ills.
We think in secret, and it comes to pass –
Environment is but our looking glass, (Allen, 1987).

HOW TO RETRAIN YOUR MIND

1. Know what you want – Be clear and specific. Focusing on too many things creates confusion.

You are thinking, *Linda, you make it sound so simple. Know what I want? Amid confusion, doubt, fear, and uncertainty during all the other times I tried, it didn't go well for me, I'm so confused…*

If this feels like where you are on a specific topic, I recommend using a journal, any journal to put your thoughts on paper. It allows you to see all the information in one place where you can process it and arrange it in a sequence that you can make sense of and create some order to the chaos. Identifying what you are afraid of and coming up with a solution. This is not about the reality you're actually dealing with, it's the unknown that is creating the fear and a way to control the fear is to look at the worst case scenario and ask yourself, "what could I do? Not what you would like to do or if it is a reasonable solution, just simply, what could I do if?" Studies show that the worst you could imagine often does not occur, but you take yourself through the emotional trauma as if it is happening now. Instead, ask yourself, "What if things went exceedingly above all I could ever ask or think? What if? If you are creating an emotional response by what you think about, why not think of things working out for you, and have that experience? This is a way to "Deconstruct Fear." Practice using this tool every time you encounter a situation that creates a negative emotion or reaction in your body.

You'll also learn a breathing technique that will help support you in how to use this approach to help you gain control of your emotions. Controlling your emotions helps you to consider how to respond proactively rather than react to something in your external environment. When doing the exercise, also consider the "Mirror Effect." The mirror effect is when you write down what you're afraid of. What thoughts come to mind that overwhelm you, almost to tears? Now breathe…now look at that scenario and think, *but what if?* What if the opposite of that happens, the other extreme?

What if you do not fail? What if you thrive in this new opportunity? What if people buy your book? What if this person is genuinely who he says he is? We are programmed to always see the glass as empty. To think positive, you must be intentional. And when you do this, notice a feeling of calm and relief begin to settle in. This continues to prove my point that your thoughts are powerful. You can think the worst of a situation and feel horrible and afraid and run back to where you're comfortable, or you can lean in and focus on the accomplishment. Focus on being in a loving, healthy, supportive relationship. The fear is first created in your mind that, in turn, triggers a physical response. That response can be positive or negative, but no matter the reaction, you control the thought. How many times have we sabotaged ourselves because we default to what's wrong as opposed to what's right?

2. Keep the main thing the main thing.

Unnecessary clutter when it comes to your thoughts can hinder the programming of innovative ideas. When you're relaxed and you're detached from the day-to-day chaos, your subconscious mind is highly receptive to suggestions. Many times, we have absorbed and stored in our memory dominant thoughts and feelings that don't serve us and we may need to deal with or seek counseling or therapy to resolve. With 60,000 thoughts a day bombarding your mind, how do you sift through to determine which ones are serving you and which ones aren't. As you are calling for the relationship that you want, and not a relationship that you could settle for, let's walk through your Relationship Genealogy. Your mother, grandmother, other women in your family. What legacy did they leave that you are unconsciously still recreating? Retrace your steps to identify patterns of behavior that you may have not made the connection to that you keep unintentionally creating and are covertly sabotaging your relationships.

3. Eliminate negative influences in your life: the news, TV programs (reality TV), social media, friends, family, or people in your workplace. This may sound extreme. I recognize that you can't divorce your family, your children, or your coworkers; however, when interacting with them threatens your mental health, your peace of mind, then it's time to create healthy boundaries that allow you to respect others and maintain your peace. Not everyone has earned the right to hear your story. Keep some things to yourself. Sometimes, you cannot share your dream or vision until it has manifested. When people can't see how (using their logic and reasoning, or perhaps they heard of or knew someone who tried to do something one time and failed) even with good intentions, they can create doubt and unbelief.

CHALLENGE: Use your *Journal*; We eat an elephant one piece at a time. Who or what might others say you're addicted to that doesn't serve you? Consider selecting something from each category, and if appropriate, create a SMART goal to help guide you toward success. S - Specific, M - Measurable, A - Achievable, R - Relevant, T - Time-Bound.

> 4. FEAR. Find the patterns of behavior that are consistent that sabotage your goals – sometimes it's your experience from the past or the experiences of others. There's a healthy innate fear known as the fight or flight response which is a physiological reaction that occurs in response to a perceived harmful event, attack, or threat to survival.

Then there's Neophobia – the fear of trying something new, especially if the fear is irrational and persistent. Growth calls forth fear. Fear of the unknown, fear of failure, also known as atychiphobia. Overcoming fear can be managed by starting small, accept that fear is normal and can be overcome, focus on what you can control, be patient with yourself, and manage your expectations. A strategy that may be helpful: Implement the tool learned, Deconstruct Fear. Fear rooted in a belief or a belief system that you must confront, whether that's a belief about money, men, women, sex, food, hair, etc. Anything that's a barrier to intimacy needs to be addressed. Anything that paralyzes you and prevents you from moving forward should be confronted. Whether there's a solution or a resolution where you make peace with the situation, what no longer is an option is to remain stagnant. Being stagnant is like a body of water having no current or flow and often having an unpleasant smell as a consequence. That's what happens in different areas of our lives. When opportunities show up and trigger our fear, or threaten to expose our pain, we deflect, avoid, project onto others the unpleasant smell of our garbage that we carry from relationship to relationship, always blaming someone or something else for our incomplete metamorphosis.

ACTION ITEM

If attempting to change your mind or behavior doesn't work just by making affirmations, how do you change your thoughts? Remember, your subconscious mind is where your habits and emotions are. To successfully accept a new idea, the most effective way is to get into a sleepy, drowsy state where you're relaxed, and slow down your breathing, which slows down the thoughts racing through your mind. Start off in small 10-15-minute increments, and your only goal initially is just to breathe and slow down your thoughts. I'm not asking you to stop thinking, just slow your thoughts down by focusing on your breathing. Some people give up because every time they decide to sit still for any length of time it feels like their thoughts go into overdrive. If you are new to this, start slow. If you fall asleep, then shift your position. Instead of lying down on your back (a sure-fire way to induce sleep, no worries, your body probably needed the additional rest), sit up, relax, and place your hands on your thighs or beside you, feet comfortably flat on the floor, or sit with your legs crossed yoga style, whatever is best for you. When your mind wanders, and it will, refocus on your breathing. I like what's called the Square Breathing Technique.

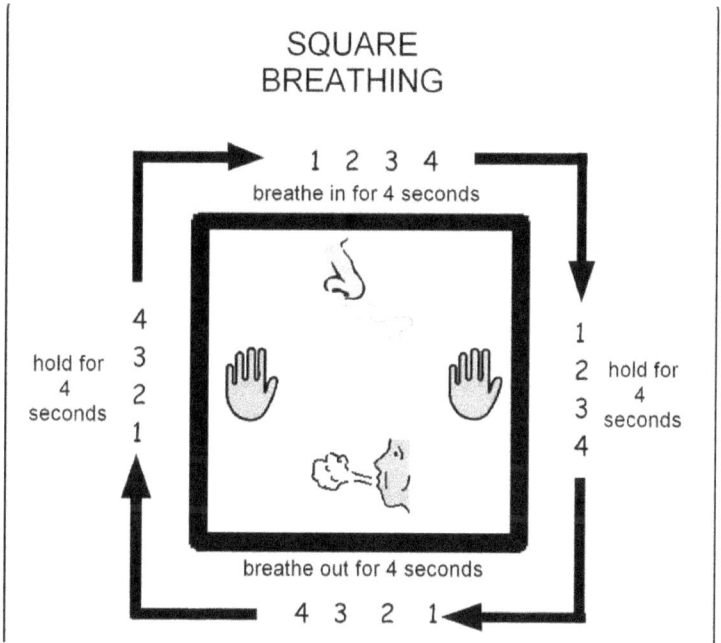

4 steps of square breathing

- Step 1: Inhale slowly through your nose while mentally counting to four. Concentrate on filling your lungs and abdomen with air. Let your body feel how air is filling your lungs.
- Step 2: Hold your breath and mentally count to four.

- Step 3: Exhale slowly through your mouth while mentally counting to four.
- Step 4: Hold your breath and mentally count to four again.

Once you've done this a few times, next, begin to make those positive affirmations or put on some headphones and listen to a Guided Meditation of positive, I AM affirmations. The mind is receptive to repetition. Once the mind accepts whatever idea is impressed upon it, it operates like a computer. It spits out what you put in it.

Meditation or the act of intentional focus or clearing your mind, depending on the type of meditation, can help you relax, reduce anxiety and stress, and more. When you're in your fully conscious awake state, and you make statements like I AM _____ (fill in the blank), but that I Am statement is so far away from what you believe, then no results manifest into physical evidence of the I AM that you state.

FACT VS TRUTH

Let us discuss the difference between facts and the truth. A fact is something that's indisputable, based on empirical research and quantifiable measures. Facts go beyond theories. They're proven through calculation and experience, or they're something that definitively occurred in the past. **Truth is entirely different; it may include fact, but it can also include belief.** Fact is indisputable. Truth is acceptable.

Your conscious, logical, reasoning mind is looking at the facts of your reality while you are trying to convince it of the truth. This approach is often an uphill battle to change. Shifting your position through meditation and using a different approach creates an advantage over your conscious mind to affect transformation.

The one thing your subconscious mind cannot do is act contrary to the conscious mind. If the conscious mind doesn't believe you, there's nothing the subconscious can do because the subconscious mind doesn't make decisions, it just carries out the commands of the conscious mind. The subconscious can't tell the difference between real or imagined. If what you feel, whether it's true or not, you believe it to be true for you, then you get what you believe.

Take for example, what you eat. We have vegan, vegetarian, pescatarian, flexitarian, and macrobiotics diets. Is there data that suggest one versus the other promotes a healthier lifestyle? I am sure, but that doesn't explain why an individual who has none of those restrictions and limitations can outlive an individual who practices any of those lifestyles or why a person who follows a strict diet, no alcohol, and runs 5 miles a day can drop dead of a heart attack. Why bother if death is inevitable? Having a body without disease or pain is more enjoyable than a body that's in distress and pain. You just feel better. When you're not comfortable in your body, it has a negative effect on the way you move and operate in this world. It affects your confidence, your self-esteem, your energy level, your joy, your peace. I'm not advocating body size or body type one over the other. What I am advocating is loving you. And if you don't feel good in the body you're in, then what can you do gradually to create new behaviors that serve you mentally and physically? What you believe about your body is true for you.

The point I'm making is that the mind is a powerful organ, and you get what you believe. This belief overrides any external force that may come against you or equally any external force that supports you. It's nice to have the love and support of others cheering you on toward your goals, but to the individual who doesn't have a positive, loving support system, I'm here to declare you can still reach your goals because the **ONLY** thing that matters is what you think about you and how you feel about whatever you desire. If there is outside influence, any power you give them or allow is the power they have to affect change in your life.

That is the difference between truth and facts. Facts are the indisputable reality; the truth is what YOU believe. To believe means you have practiced a thought so succinctly that despite what you see, you still believe (Faith). Flip Wilson (I'm telling my age), used to always say, "What you see is what you get." The truth is, what you believe is what you get, and that doesn't require physical sight, just your imagination.

Many years ago, I used to drive a 2005 Mercedes-Benz C230 Kompressor Sports Coupe, candy apple red with black leather interior and a black spoiler on the back. It was fun to drive until I started liking BMWs. I decided I wanted a BMW, but I didn't know anything about BMWs. So, I went to a dealership and told the guy I wanted to buy a BMW, but I didn't know much about them. He was more than happy to give me a history lesson on the different make and models and even let me test drive the 3-series and 7-series. Over the next few days and maybe a week or so later, as I obsessed over this BMW, I remember sweeping out my 1-car garage and walking out into the garage and imagining my beautiful new BMW being in the garage. I would walk around the space as if I were walking around the BMW. I felt so proud of myself. Within 10 days, my Alpine White BMW 325i with Terra interior (looks like the color of a football) was in my garage just as I had imagined 2 weeks prior. This is not only how I AM works, but this is exactly how thoughts turn to things. The Universe can only manifest what you believe. If you believe there is a shortage of good, available men who want to be in a committed relationship, then the men who are attracted to you are the emotionally unavailable men you believe to exist.

Why am I going through this exhaustive explanation of how the mind works? Because the way you think, and feel is everything. It's the key to unlock the door to your Ideal Mate; the key to your finances, the key to your health, the key to your career and other business ventures, EVERYTHING. Whatever area you're experiencing can be traced back to a thought or a limiting belief created at some point in your life that you may or may not have a memory of. For some people, it's not just one limiting belief; it's a belief system, a way of thinking and being in the world about relationships, money, marriage, business, etc.

STOP

Go back to the beginning of the chapter titled, Quantum Leap and read this again to ensure there are no cracks in your foundation. If you need to, do the practice again, and again and again. This is an opportunity to really shine the light on the shadows of darkness that are getting in the way of your partnership. These are foundational principles that are like building blocks. A builder would never start building without clearing the land where they lay the foundation. Put a marker on this page and go back to the beginning of Quantum Leap. If you're not in a relationship or are casually dating, just check yourself. Are there any fears or concerns you have about being all in? What's coming up for you at this moment? If you're in a serious relationship or married, what's going on with you that's making you question whether this is where you should be? What's causing you to slow down and reevaluate your position? What are you not getting, and what are you giving that's leaving you unfulfilled? If you don't grasp how your thoughts turn to things, how what you believe matters, it will sabotage your relationship. The key to having anything is imagining it now. Not one day, not some day, but if I had received, achieved what I want, how would I feel, and if you don't even know what you want, then you must go back to the beginning. Maybe you just need to have some renovations done, and for others, the outside may look good, but they must gut the inside and start over. Before you move forward, just take a moment and breathe. Inhale for 4 seconds and exhale for 6 seconds. Just take your time… It is a lot to process, but you are doing amazing. You got this… Breathe….

THE TERROR BARRIER

> *"Life begins at the end of your Comfort Zone"*
>
> - Neale Walsh

The Terror Barrier is a concept that represents an invisible border of your making. When you decide to make changes in your life, anxiety and fear overtake you. As these negative thoughts overwhelm you whenever you decide to go to the next level or try something different, the terror barrier is there waiting for you. Understand what's happening in your mind and in your body. To grow, you're going to have to step outside your comfort zone. Bob Proctor refers to a goal or things that you really want or things that you haven't yet experienced as a "C-type Goal." This is a goal that

1. Causes you to stretch and go beyond where you've ever been.
2. It's so big, it scares and excites you at the same time.
3. You have absolutely no idea **HOW** to reach it; you just know you will.

The problem you face is that you can't see the **HOW** or figure it out. At that moment you come face-to-face with the Terror Barrier. The worry, doubt, fear, and anxiety can be paralyzing. When this happens, you're left with two choices:

1. Go back to safety.
2. Push through the fear and remain in pursuit of the goal.

Most people choose to go back to safety, what's known, because the fear of what they might lose is too great.

What's really going on, and why is it important to the Strategic Relationship Plan? An idea originates in the conscious mind, the part that can accept or reject it. A C-type goal is not just an idea but a feeling around that new idea. The subconscious mind must accept everything you believe. Belief is the repetition of rehearsing what it looks like and feels like that's true for you. Your actions are consistent with the belief, the way you speak is aligned with what you believe, the way you move in the world is propelled by the thoughts and actions toward what you want that you believe is yours. Your subconscious mind cannot differentiate between what's real and what's imagined. If your conscious mind accepts your idea (C-type goal), impresses it on the subconscious mind, the subconscious mind accepts it as true right away, and the manifestation is inevitable.

The subconscious is the seat of your emotions, the storehouse of your memories. The subconscious mind determines the vibration that your body is in, which affects how you feel. In your comfort zone, your thoughts and beliefs are aligned in what I call X-type thinking. When you move into the realm of a new idea, which I call a Y-idea, and start to act on it, the subconscious mind, with the old program of X-type thinking, rejects it. It is like mixing oil and water. Your central nervous system is overtaken by fear and anxiety, and your natural reaction is to seek shelter in what's familiar. You retreat, go back. The next time you are ready to do something different, make a change and recognize what's happening. It is going to happen. What can you do about it?

1. Recognize that you're simply introducing a new idea "Y" that doesn't fit with the old idea of yourself "X."
2. Rather than getting stuck doing what you've always done, lean into the uncomfortable, the unfamiliar, and keep impressing the new idea

on the subconscious mind with gratitude and faith.

3. Keep pushing until the unfamiliar becomes familiar.

Fear and growth go hand in hand. I had a friend tell me once that Fear is just an indication that it's time to move to the next level. Everything you want is on the other side of fear. So, push through the Terror Barrier, push through the fear, and, in a relatively short time, you'll break through the barrier, the resistance, into a new reality. You have made what was once unfamiliar – familiar, uncomfortable – comfortable.

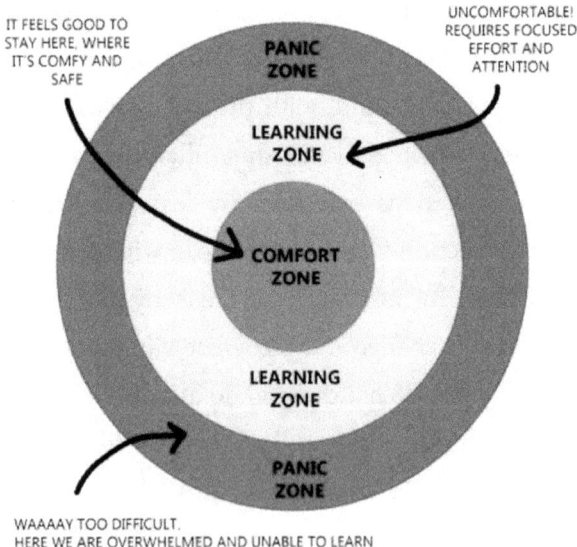

Diagram courtesy of Claudia Kaier

Please tread lightly when dealing with emotional wounds. Like physical wounds, there are stages of healing.

While open, it's very sensitive to being touched by anything directly or indirectly. But to heal, sometimes, the medicine stings, tastes bad, or, if not protected, can cause an infection, or reinjure the wound. Be easy with your heart. Avoiding the pain delays the healing. For deep trauma, do not play the hero. Seek help. How do you know if you're in growth mode or treacherous and dangerous territory? If you're in the growth zone, you'll feel some anxiety, but you'll also feel excitement at the same time. The terror zone feels like panic, feels like fear, feels like overwhelm, even pain. Excitement is nowhere in the terror zone. To push forward causes you to traumatize yourself all over again, creating more fear and putting another roadblock in your way. As you go through the healing process, when you can slowly expose yourself to the trigger and have a different response shows just how far you've come. In some instances, going back may not be necessary. Let the past stay in the past if it's not hindering your future.

If you got this far and are excited to learn more, I celebrate you. Before you can start building, you must prepare the soil. Understanding how your mind works and what happens in your body when you entertain a thought or imagine something different is invaluable to your ability to succeed in love and in life. Absorb these principles as food for the soul and there's nothing you can't do, be, or have.

What To Expect

I'll follow a business plan template as the structure of this blueprint and modify the language to correlate to what resonates within the community of intimate relationships. Language is critical to our ability to create alignment. This book was written for the woman who has achieved some level of success in business or career yet is often challenged with finding that same level of success when it comes to having a healthy, loving, thriving partnership.

You may not have written a business plan, but the concept is relatable to all women. The blueprint is to help give form and fashion to the creation of your Ideal Mate, your

Partnership. Writing down what you want is simply an exercise in focus and attention. If you give it enough attention, you create a magnetic field around you that will attract what you are. The creation of the relationship plan will require you to become what you seek. The Dalai Lama said, "If you do not love yourself, you cannot love others." Developing the blueprint is the knowledge, applying the information is the power that activates the manifestation, but without love, knowledge and power won't lead to happiness.

The principles you'll learn in this book are to remind you of who you are born to become. The principles taught in this book are based on the Law of Assumption with remnants of the Law of Attraction delivered in a way that brings about transformation in your relationship quest. Take your time. This is all about you. Read this information as many times as you need too. Remember, anytime you introduce a new idea into your consciousness, the body treats it like a foreign object and immediately has an allergic reaction. Not because it's not achievable, but because the conscious, logical reasoning mind tries to figure out how to make it happen. What you have done in that moment is send a signal to your subconscious mind that activates the fight or flight response to protect you from the emotional stress you're creating. Our approach blocks our ability to be successful in that desire or, at least, make it harder to get what we want. What if I could offer you a different approach that would bypass your conscious mind, the gatekeeper of the subconscious mind, and deliver powerful, positive suggestions that the subconscious would receive so that when you begin to see yourself in a happy, loving, compatible long-term relationship, that which you believe to be true is what manifests in your physical reality?

Chapter 1

COMPANY DESCRIPTION

"If you limit your choices only to what seems possible or reasonable, you disconnect yourself from what you truly want, and all that is left is a compromise." - Robert Fritz

This section explains the basic elements of your business and the simple or complex nature of you. This is one of the most challenging elements of the relationship plan. This may be something you develop over the course of days, weeks, even months. To help guide you to a compelling and effective mission statement, I have relied heavily on the work done by James Collins and William Lazier in their book *Beyond Entrepreneurship* to draw distinctions between mission and vision.

Understand the difference between your mission and your vision

Companies often use "vision statement" and "mission statement" interchangeably. There is a difference. Vision comprises three things: your core values, your purpose, and your mission. In essence, your mission can be birthed from your vision.

Vision encompasses:

- *Core Values.* Your core values and beliefs are your guiding philosophy, the fundamental tenets that shape what your business should be.
- *Purpose.* Your purpose is tightly connected to the core values and is, basically, your company's reason for existence.
- *Mission.* Your mission is your company's clear and compelling goal that serves as a focal point of effort.

The concept of core values is usually easy to grasp. They are derived *not* from asking what core values *you should* hold but what core values you *do* hold. The difference between purpose and mission is more elusive. Your **purpose** is like a guiding star, you always strive for it, fixate on it, but you never actually reach the star. It's what you constantly strive to attain, your reason for being.

Your **mission** is the mountain you're currently climbing to reach closer to the star. Once you get over the mountain, you refocus on your guiding star, head toward it, and choose another mountain to climb. Your mission is what you intend to become or accomplish; it should be challenging but achievable.

Although core values, purpose, and mission were familiar terms, I had never actually sat down and identified clearly what those were for me. Oh yeah, telling the truth and respect were important, but when I looked at my previous relationships, I had not defined my core values as a statement of who I am. Hence, I compromised, made excuses, and tolerated behavior that I now would not hesitate to walk away from.

Use your journal to vet your ideas and craft your Mission Statement:

How to begin crafting your Mission statement

- What are your core values and beliefs? What do you believe in your gut?
- What is your purpose for being? Why does your company exist? Ask "why" seven times to get to your core purpose, your ultimate reason for what you came to contribute to the world.
- What's the immediate hurdle you must overcome to move you closer to your purpose?

The act of writing a mission statement can be difficult. You can approach the process from a few angles.

Tap the creative genius inside

Capturing the essence of your business on paper will challenge your creative genius. Here's a mission-statement-creation exercise that asks questions that encourage an emotional response, for example, how do you feel?) The words and phrases generated tend to be more meaningful when they describe emotions. Questions from the brainstorming process include:

- Imagine you are your life partner who has just had an encounter with you while waiting in line to get into an event, a concert, a restaurant, etc. What are the first words that come to mind?
- You're walking downtown and see a couple, holding hands and heading to the same restaurant you're headed to for lunch. The woman looks just like you, confident, smiling, glowing. She looks happy. He opens the door for her and escorts her in by her waist signaling to everyone that she's with him. It is complete. As you observe them, describe what you see.
- When you value yourself, when you realize you have something to offer that's of value to others, it's like giving them a gift. What are you giving your ideal mate, your ideal relationship?

These exercise questions prod you to see the world from a different vantage point.

- Use descriptive, powerful, and active words. Avoid formulaic, jargon-heavy language.
- Be clear and concise.
- Be honest and realistic.
- Communicate expectations and ethics.

From conception to completion

Your statement may go through several stages of revision. After each work session, put it away for a few hours or days.

Tweak it as necessary, incorporate feedback from others if you like, but it is not necessary. Remember, a mission statement is a brief explanation of your company's reason for being. A mission statement concisely defines the company's reason for being and its core values… it's a "why" statement… and defines in general terms how a company makes the world a better (or different) place.

Company philosophy and vision

a. What values does the relationship live by? *Honesty, integrity, fun, innovation,* and *community* are examples of values that might be important to your business philosophy. Core values are traits or qualities that are not just worthwhile, they represent an individual's or an organization's highest priorities, deeply held beliefs, and core, fundamental driving forces.
b. *Vision* refers to the long-term outlook for your business. What do you want it to become? What is your legacy?

When it comes to attracting a life partner, why is it important to know what your core values and beliefs are? One reason relationships fail is because core values are not aligned. What does that mean? If integrity and high moral character are important to you, doing business with a company that takes advantage of others, always trying to get one over on the system and manipulating a situation to serve their agenda can destroy YOUR company. To tolerate and make excuses damages your foundation, not theirs. What do you believe in? This is not to imply that you all must agree on all issues or topics, but there must be a fundamental agreement on the things that are important to you.

Real life example: I was in a relationship with a person who looked down on others he thought had less value than himself. Subsequently, he was rude to people who waited on us at restaurants. If someone didn't have a title, he was disrespectful simply because he thought he was better than everyone else. He would embellish stories just to make himself look good and because his image was everything. He would say all the right things to impress others whose opinions he cared about but lived contrary to that which he spoke. It took a long time to dissolve that partnership, but what I knew for sure, liking the person was equally as important as loving that person. How you treat others is important to me not just when others are looking but when no one is looking.

Why do we tolerate immoral behavior? Why do we make excuses for failure? Why is holding others and often us accountable hard to do? Do you think a business can continue to grow if you have leaders who don't lead? If you don't care about the growth of your company, how do you expect others to care about the growth of your company? If it's not important to you, should it be important to others?

- **Company goals**

Specify your long- and short-term goals as well as any milestones or benchmarks you'll use to measure your progress.

It doesn't matter where you are in life, you should continue to have goals. Goals provide direction. Goals have purpose. Purpose gives you a reason for being. The Harvard Study showed that the chances of you obtaining your goal increase significantly when you have a goal and increase exponentially when you write those goals down and spend a few minutes creating a mental image with emotion of what it feels like to have reached that goal.

My intention for identifying a goal is not to become ritualistic, but to define a destination, something to focus on or move toward. Knowing where you're going is half the battle. Being equipped to make the journey is the other half. What are your goals? List at least three to five short term and three to five long-term goals. To help you get started, here are five key areas to focus on:

- Health
- Career
- Finances
- Spirituality/Faith
- Family/friends/relationships

This doesn't mean you have to focus on everything at the same time, but identifying areas you would like to improve in or create gives you direction. When you program your destination using GPS, you can always add another destination to your route, but you can't have too many stops along the way. Once you have arrived at one destination you can always add another stop or change your destination all together if you need to. Whether you're using Waze or Google Maps, you must know where you want to go, and because there's rarely a straight line between where you are and where you want to be, each of us has a built-in Global Problem Solver (GPS) that knows how to get us to wherever we want to go if you know where you want to end up.

- *Legal Structure – What is your relationship status?*

    a. Are you single, divorced, consciously uncoupling (meaning it is an amicable separation)? Is it complicated?

*****Class in Session**: Did you know the law of physics states that no two objects can occupy the same space at the same time? If someone still resides in your heart and in your mind, you're not ready for what you say you want. Back in the day, it was called "Soul-Ties." That emotional connection was so strong that breaking away from that person seemed impossible. They would haunt every relationship you would attempt to have moving forward. Are you looking for reparations from the new relationship? Is this person paying for the past sins of others? What are you holding onto from your past that's preventing you from moving into your future?

Questions?
1. Do you still think about your ex?
2. Do you still talk about your ex to whomever will tolerate the conversation?
3. Do you compare everybody to your ex?
4. Is your ex still like a member of the family?
5. Do you scrutinize and compare your ex's new mate to yourself?
6. Do you still care what your ex does with other people?
7. Do you still think about your ex and have a negative or positive reaction to something he did or said that happened in the past?

If you've recently dissolved a relationship, then these are signs that you're not ready to move on. If we let the dead bury the dead, then why are you resurrecting a dead relationship? Every time you give attention to the past, it's like giving mouth-to-mouth resuscitation, and you wonder why you feel shitty when you narrate what happened. Until you've made peace with that person, that relationship, it will be a threat to your new relationship. Listen, I get it. My ex-husband had me in court for five years over custody. He didn't really want custody, he just wanted to hurt me. It was a power move. Five years and $30,000 dollars later, and he only got what I was willing to give. That didn't compensate me for the emotional and physical toll that going to court and listening to my character being assassinated to prove I'm an unfit mother had on me. In eighteen years, paternity was never questioned until child support was petitioned. Every tactic legally available he used, not because he thought he could win but to torture me for leaving. These principles that you're learning, the exercises you're being asked to do are designed to handle whatever you must go through to get to the other side. Winston Churchill said, "If you're going through hell, keep going."

Even after war there is a debriefing. When you're coming out of a relationship, take a minute to exhale that old relationship. Do a debriefing. In the context of the relationship strategy, take a minute to ask yourself some questions for the purpose of G&D, (Growth & Development).

1. Am I ready?

Does my lifestyle support the time and energy necessary to invest in a relationship?

2. Am I really over my ex?

If you say yes, but you are secretly hoping you'll get back together, know that rebound relationships are destined to fail. You are already building a foundation on the sand of a lie. It's a myth that perpetuates the wrong idea that the best way to get over an ex is to be with the next. The best way to get over an ex is to work on YOU.

3. What didn't work in my previous relationship(s)?

Make a list.

4. What did work?

Identify the positive aspects of the relationship that you can carry into your next relationship.

5. What kind of relationship do I want?

If you find that in describing what kind of relationship you want is a list of all the things you do not want based on all the negative things that happened in your previous relationship, this is a red flag. Knowing what you don't want is not the same as recognizing what you do want. The key is to turn your attention to what you do want and stop telling the story of what you don't want. This is subtle but makes a huge difference in getting what you want. What you give your attention to, you get more of.

6. Do we have shared core values?

The more commonality of core values in a relationship the smoother the approach to solving life challenges when they arise. For example, monogamy. If that's something you value but they don't, no matter how many other things you may love about that person, this will present a problem in the relationship. If your partner values solitude, but you value companionship, the closer you move to them, the more they step away. This can be worked on, but it will require more effort than if you both valued companionship.

7. What do I want out of a relationship?

The work you're doing in developing a relationship plan will help you to be clear about this objective BEFORE you enter a new relationship.

8. Do I love myself?

Self-love means having a high regard for your own well-being and happiness. Self-love means taking care of your own needs and not sacrificing your well-being to please others. Self-love means not settling for less than you deserve. Not loving yourself means that you have a hard time accepting love from another, and that unintentional rejection can strain the relationship because you're sabotaging the love you want with your inability to receive love. Love is a two-way street. Some people can give love to others but are uncomfortable receiving love. For example, do you feel uncomfortable when others compliment you, celebrate you, put you in the spotlight?

9. What characteristics am I looking for in a partner?

Confidence? Sense of humor? Humility? Kindness? Motivation? Work ethic? Supportive? Does your potential partner embody most of the characteristics that you want in a partner?

10. Does this person bring out the best in me?

Respite is a brief period of rest or relief from something difficult or unpleasant, such as a bad relationship. When you don't go on a respite, you often make quick decisions and date people just because you're bored or you don't want to be alone. How do you feel when you're with this person? How do you behave? Are you able to be your authentic self? There are some great people out there; they just may not be great for you.

Who you date says more about you than it does about them. You attract who you are, not what you want. If you are not ready for the responsibility of a committed relationship, then own that and be honest with the individuals you encounter. Sometimes, you've been in a relationship for so long that being single is uncomfortable, so you jump into another relationship right away without respite. Consider your past as research and the experience(s) as necessary to gather more information to become clearer about what you want. Those experiences may feel like they happened to you, but I come to unveil the truth. Those experiences happened for you. How would you discover strength without adversity? How do you recognize a great partner if you have never had one that wasn't so great? All things work together for your good, all things.

To give you a little insight into what's happening in your brain, it's common to struggle in this area because of a drug-like substance the brain produces when you're in love called "dopamine." Unfortunately, memories of love, and things that have happened during and after the relationship are often distorted because research shows (Luchies et al., 2013) that those who trust their partners remember the bad things their partners did more positively than those with low trust. What that means is, being in love with a person even after the relationship ends can cause a distortion in how you remember the events that took place in the relationship. So, blame it on the dopamine, the feel-good hormone the brain releases when you experience pleasure. But not even dopamine can override your decision to not give your attention to an individual or replay of an event that caused you pain once you make that conscious decision internally. Are you willing to allow whatever happened in your past to continue to rob you of your joy today?

Life Principle: Whatever you focus on grows. If you want something to die, don't give it your attention. Stop talking about, stop agreeing with others with the same sad story, delete the pictures, get rid of things that remind you of them. All that stuff carries energy and sometimes, change requires courage. The courage to let go so you can move on. Pivot! And with a little bit of effort, step-by-step you'll walk yourself out of that pit and one day the thought will just be a thought. A thought with no power, suddenly. Starting can sometimes be the most difficult step you'll take.

Legal Structure continued....

    a. Do you have Investors, meaning children? Are you a single parent? Are you the primary custodian or the noncustodial parent? What are the custody arrangements? How old are the children? How involved is the other parent? Describe the coparenting relationship. How do you and when is the best time to introduce your children to your potential life partner? This can be tricky. This is an ongoing conversation with your potential partner and will require some manipulation of events to slowly introduce this new person into your investors' lives. Equally important, if this person is a part of your life and there is going to be a change in the organizational structure, how will this impact your investors' needs to be strategic?

This topic of Investors could be its own chapter; however, this interaction requires some strategy. I don't have a timetable of when this introduction is right, but I do think it needs to be vetted. Every child has their own temperament, but communicate, communicate, communicate leading up to this introduction. And if it's slow and steady and you can integrate your partner into the structure, that's great. There are no perfect scenarios, but with caution, thought, and strategic planning, do the best you can to assure your children that they're not being replaced, sacrificed, or make them feel neglected because of this relationship. Children very rarely like the idea of you dating, and you're not looking for approval but cooperation. If they're dealing with the trauma of the loss of the other parent in any way, talk to your children, create an environment, a time where and when they have your full attention to listen. If the company will be experiencing separation or a dissolution of the current structure, continue to build a bridge that will support your investors through this transition. Children are unique individuals with their own set of challenges, adding the idea of a new person into their environment or changing their existing environment requires strategy.

After reading the Company Description, you should have a basic understanding of your business's mission, vision, goals, and legal structure.

Chapter 2
MARKET ANALYSIS

Your business development plan must start with a detailed summary of who your target customers are and what their wants and needs are.

Without this understanding, you cannot speak directly to your customers. What that means in the realm of a relationship is defined as "What do you want?" Targeting in the context of a relationship has to do with "energy."

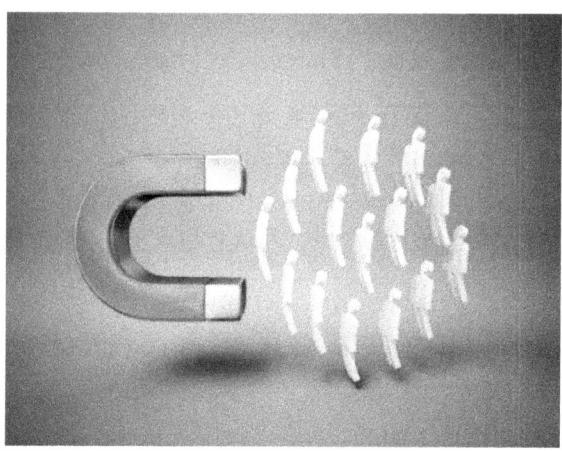

YOUR MIND IS A MAGNET

The secret to manifesting your desire is not just in giving attention to something or someone; it's in the energy and emotion of the desire. If you give a lot of attention with the emotion of wanting, your subconscious interprets that as "I lack," and it will perpetuate that lack. But if you give a little attention with the emotion of gratitude, imagining that you have what you desire, your subconscious will manifest it because you're saying, "I have."

Unfortunately, for most people, the thing they really, really want has so much energy associated with it because they've been thinking about it for a long time, they've wanted it for a long time, so it's hard to not care if they don't get it. And often, when you've been wanting something for a long time, it's natural to notice how long it's taking and have resistance to plead your case of all the things you've done or are doing to manifest this thing you want, resistance to get weary, resistance to wonder if this thing you want will ever happen for you, resistance.... These are all normal, natural, human reactions. I've heard people say, "It wasn't until I gave up on wanting this thing that it came to me." Well, what happens is they give up the resistance. They got to a point where they decided to be happy even if this thing they wanted never happened. If you've put a part of your life on hold waiting for your life partner to show up, then yeah, it's going to be a while. Why? Because being happy isn't dependent on your life partner. You have to be happy now, life is amazing now, and your life is full now. And the very moment you realize you don't need your life partner to fill a void in your life is when they show up. It absolutely blows your mind. And there is one other thing. Remember, I said that this is a very personal and spiritual journey. You cannot fool the Universe. You can fool me, you can fool people, you can put on a mask, you can say all the right words, but the Universe isn't listening to what you say; it's listening to how you feel.

If you don't know what you want, in your journal, write down all the things that you don't want. Next to each statement write the opposite or positive counterpart to the negative statement. Also, the word "want" implies lack. So, in the positive statement, replace it with "desire." For example:

- I don't want a man who cheats – I desire a man who is faithful and monogamous.
- I don't want a man who lies – I desire a man who is honest.
- I don't want a man who is needy – I desire a man who is secure, confident.

The exercise is designed to get you to focus on what you want, and this can be a challenge for some people because they know what they don't want and that's what they focus on with passion not realizing that they get what they focus on. Do not get stuck in the weeds. You came to visit not to stay. I won't mention any names; however, there's a musical artist who was married and divulged during an interview with a magazine that she didn't allow her husband to have female friends or work with other female artists. She believed this was a strategy to keep him from cheating. What rules do you have in place, what threats or ultimatums have you issued that ever kept anyone from doing what you didn't want them to do? How did that work out for you? Don't you know you can't legislate behavior. If we could, we would not need prisons. Fidelity is about the character of the individual and not the nature of the business they're in. Let's place responsibility where it needs to be. Monogamy is a choice. It doesn't mean you're not tempted; it means you're mature enough to decide what's more important to you. What do you value more?

Class In Session: There's no such thing as "No" in the subconscious. When you say "Yes" to something, you get it. When you say "No" to something, it's like saying "Yes." I don't want a man who lies to me. What do you get? A man who lies to you. Why? Because the Universe translates "I do not want" to "Yes, give me more, even if it's not what I want." There is no such thing as "No." Crazy, right? When you're complaining about what you don't have or how long it's taking to get what you want. The Universe hears "Yes, I want more of that lack and waiting." Observe the patterns in your life, in your relationships. Wonder why you keep attracting the same type of men, friends, similar experiences? This works positively as well. I know it sounds nuts, counterintuitive to logic. The Universe is not logical.

Think about being a magnet in the Universe with an energy field around you, attracting not what you say but the strong, often silent ultrasonic energy that is vibrating at an elevated level, attracting things into your physical experience. The world sees the effects of your thoughts, not the cause. Wonder why bad things happen to good people? This explains the adage, don't judge a book by its cover. You can't know for sure what a person is thinking or feeling at any given time. That is why suicide is so tragic. We see the effects; they look happy and successful, yet in the darkness, they're in pain. The mask of conformity dies a slow death in the shadows. In life, we should strive for harmony because balance is often unrealistic.

What we are living today is the effect of our thoughts and feelings. Most people live in their past, not their future. What you experience today is a direct result of a culmination of thoughts and feelings that have gathered a lot of momentum because of your attention to them. And every time you relive those yesterdays, they create your today. And today looks like yesterday and the day before and the day before that. If you don't change the way you're thinking it's easy to see how depression sets in because it feels like nothing is changing when, in fact, things are changing; it's just that they're changing to more of the same.

You break the cycle when you live in the imagination of your future because those thoughts and feelings create hope and expectation. When you begin to act like you already have the thing you desire, the level of energy in your brain and body elevates. When you believe that you already have what you desire, then the subconscious gives you more of what you have because your thoughts are on appreciating the love you have, so it gives you more love. When you live with an abundance mindset, you believe that you have more than enough, so the subconscious gives you more…more money, more love, more joy, more peace, more, more, more.

The same is true for our ego. Ego is defined as a person's sense of self-esteem or self-importance. I believe anything out of balance can cause harm, even something as good and essential to who we are, which is our ego. The ego can magnify either our best or worst side. In relationships, the ego thinks the best way to love someone is to change them; so, the effort to love, through the filter of the ego, becomes the need to control.

When you come to know who you are, there will be no need for hierarchy in the relationship. There will be no need to control or change your partner. Do the work, and insecurity, which is often a trigger to lack, will not threaten to destroy the partnership that you are committed to building.

Now that you've taken some time to jot down the things you like and the things you don't like, let's put those thoughts together to begin imagining the man/woman uniquely created just for you.

How to develop your partner's profile:

A. Demographic Profile
(Note that not all these demographic criteria may be relevant to your company. Ignore ones that are not relevant. Add any to the list that might be missing.)

Geographic Location:

Age range:

Income:

Gender:

Nationality/Ethnicity:

Marital Status:

Household Size:

Occupation/Employment status:

Industry:

Language:

Education:

Political tendencies:

Other:

B. PSYCHOGRAPHIC PROFILE

Describe the psychographic profile of your partner. What do they do for fun? What TV shows do they watch? What do they believe in? What are they enthusiastic about?

Activities

Interests

Opinions

Attitudes

Values

C. *Your Detailed Partner Profile*

Based on your answers above, write down your detailed customer profile below.

An example may look something like this: My Ideal Partner is a single man/woman aged 45 to 65, making

6-figures or more per year, living in Manhattan, whose children are grown, likes and/or owns a pet, really cares about the environment, enjoys watching and playing sports, who is emotionally and physically available and wants to be in a relationship.

Unique Selling Proposition (USP)

Having a strong Unique Selling Proposition (USP) is another important element of your marketing plan. A USP is different from a mission statement, but typically will be reflected within your mission statement.

Your USP separates your product or service from your competitors. It makes your product or service a "unique, must have" item. The One created just for you is looking for you. Authenticity. An original. Whatever your quirks and idiosyncrasies are that make you – You. I used to iron my sheets and pillowcases. I traveled 90% of the time in my previous role and had become accustomed to fresh sheets and pillowcases staying in 4-star hotels. Before I raised my sheet game, if my sheets and pillowcases had wrinkles, I would iron them first. (I have OCD-like tendencies). My husband saw this one day when we were dating, and he was so impressed by this he knew I was the one. I do not like clutter and I really like things organized and in their places. I love to cook. I like action movies and old school rap and R&B. I am a strategist, and I know business. That was right up my husband's alley.

We love the same movies, food, sports, and music, and we both understand business and dabble in the stock market. These are things that I did or had an interest in before he showed up. It just so happened, he did too. USP doesn't have to be some major gift or talent that you possess; sometimes, it's the little things that uniquely position you for your next chapter, that's a perfect fit for your Ideal Partner. A great USP will be a magnet in and of itself that will increase your marketability and increase your conversion rates.

Follow these steps to identify your USP:

Describe the key values and/or benefits that you bring to the table that will add value to the partnership. Reinvent yourself!

Branding

Branding is defined as the process of creating a distinct identity for a business in the mind of the consumer. When we focus on the business of you, you are unique, and your personality adds to that distinct identity. So many people are trying to imitate others rather than defining who they are. Brand marketing is the process of establishing and growing a relationship between a brand and its customers. When you show up as your authentic self, the relationship is being established on what's real, honest, and open. Being your authentic self is more sustainable than being an imitation of someone else. If you don't like who you are, you could change or alter aspects of your appearance, even personality, or you could love and accept the way you are. You get to choose, and you are the only one who can. How does this apply to your relationship strategy? Think of it this way. When you think of the people who know you or know about you, what would they say if asked to describe you? What kind of person would they say you are? You may have to step outside your comfort zone and solicit this information. Why is this important? You want to make sure that the perception aligns with who you are. As a company, you are a brand. How you show up in the world matters. Are you the kind of person if someone wants to know what's going on, they call you? Are you always on the phone gossiping about things that are none of your business? Can you keep a secret? Is drama attracted to you wherever you go? Is this what your brand stands for? Either you create your brand, or the world will create one for you.

This is not about being fake or pretending to be something you're not; it's designed to allow you to decide who you want to be or who you want to become and live in the truth of who you are. Loving who you are attracts those who will love who you are. No change is required, but you and you must align first. Before some of you take this out of context, if you got a fucked-up attitude, then yes, you need to check that. Treat people the way you want to be treated. If you're a taker and never a giver, then yes, you need to check your motives. Those are not partnership characteristics.

Final USP - Take your answers to questions 1-2 and create a paragraph that portrays your unique selling proposition.

These suggestions are for those companies in the start-up phase of their business or under construction.

DISTRIBUTION PLAN

(Does not apply to existing corporations)

In the context of a relationship strategy, how will your potential ideal mate find you? Are you positioned to be found? You can't complain about not meeting single, eligible, available men if you never leave the house.

- What have you tried in the past that worked well that positions you to be asked out on a date?
- What did not work so well?
- Where have you made yourself available?
- What people do you know who could introduce you to a nice guy? Double date so it is not so awkward.
- When was the last time you got all dolled up to go out and have fun? When was the last time you did anything fun? What could you do differently? Go to www.meetup.com to find groups in your area with the same interest.
- Rebrand yourself into the woman you want to be and stop waiting for permission.

Direct Distributions Methods Used:

Will you distribute to them indirectly using friends, families, coworkers, and social media presence? Leveraging Facebook, Twitter, LinkedIn, Instagram, etc. is an extremely effective way to stay in, maintain, and grow your network, and to identify new opportunities. A creative yet disciplined approach to maintaining a persistent presence via these channels will ensure that your company's brand remains visible and front-of-mind to potential partnerships.

Identify Indirect Distributions Methods Used:

Improve Potential Prospects Perceptions of You

How others perceive you will influence whether they want to do business with you. Previously, we discussed creating your desired brand positioning. Well, this positioning must be consistent with how others view you when they are in your presence.

We all have stories of meeting someone's representative. Why not show up as the best version of you. The work to imitate others and to sustain that persona can be detrimental to your mental health. What are you afraid of? When you like who you are, would you rather be with someone who likes you with all your flaws and idiosyncrasies? Listen, show me a person who is perfect, and I will show you the flaws in that diamond. Despite the illusion of perfection on social media, what humans crave is connection. What is real? Stop asking others to tolerate something in you that you don't like. What couples have in common enables them to weather the storms of life. Chemistry may be what attracts you to a person, but compatibility is what sustains the relationship.

Chemistry vs. Compatibility

To touch on this topic lightly, you need both. The challenge is having the right mixture. Chemistry is the visceral reaction we have to another person that excites us, the feeling of wanting to connect, that desire for intimacy, and the hunger for sexual exploration. Compatibility is that confidence that comes from shared values, hopes, and dreams of building a life together. You can have one without the other, but it often does not manifest into long-term partnerships. Without chemistry, one may lose that desire for closeness and intimacy, and without compatibility, one may lose the confidence and respect for the other person, the trust that you have each other's back no matter what. It's not something you can fake, but it's always better to be cautious of the excitement in the beginning because you don't want to be hypnotized and not see the obvious signs when what's important to you is misaligned and your values and goals are very different.

Joint Ventures & Partnerships

Here's the value in having a tribe, a network.

In research from Sharpe (2022), some of the most common ways for people to meet:
- Volunteer

- Book Clubs/Bookstore
- Join a sports team
- Networking events
- Travel
- Local bars
- Go to the gym
- At Sports/Religion/Hobby Events
- On the Internet and Dating Apps
- Through family & friends
- School
- Walk your dog
- Social media
- Local hike
- Attend a music festival
- Take a course or a class
- A friend's wedding

Referral Strategy

Like Partnerships and Joint Ventures, a referral strategy uses leverage to inexpensively expand your network. But while Partnerships and Joint Ventures leverage another company's network, a referral strategy leverages your network. Referrals, as you might expect, are simply asking existing personal or professional relationships about someone they may know who someone might be you should meet

While referral systems are a great way to inexpensively use your existing contacts to meet potential prospects, optimizing your referral system is a lot deeper than simply asking if your network knows anyone whom you could connect with that meets the criteria that would potentially complement your company.

Document the referral system that you'll use:
The First Step:
The first step is common sense: get referrals. However, getting referrals is a lot more complicated than it sounds.

There are several things you need to consider and plan for if you want to maximize both the number and quality of the referrals you receive.

The person must want to do it

This is one very common problem a company has: getting their network to want to give them referrals. Why? The underlying reason may be if it doesn't work out, they don't want to jeopardize their relationship with you or the other person. However, if you have a pretty good relationship, and people want to see you happy, they may give a disclaimer and still support you anyway. Please make sure you have vetted the people you reach out to for assistance. Be confident that they're wanting what's in your best interest.

Give it more than one shot

A big problem that many companies have when it comes to getting referrals is asking more than once.

You need to be persistent without badgering anyone.

You do not have to ask over and over until you get one, but you may have some in your network whom you've worked with in the past and are fond of, and they would have liked to support you, but they didn't have any qualified prospects to refer to you.

With social media, it's easier to stay in touch, and you can message them privately if you want to follow up.

Do not stop at one

Here's another mistake that most companies make: only having one referral system.

If you have a network, you can ask them directly for referrals. That is easy.

You should brainstorm all the points where you contact individuals in your network and social clubs and consider how you can use them to get a referral from them (while also keeping the next item in mind).

Timing is everything

One thing that's going to kill the number of referrals you receive is bad timing. Don't ask for a referral if you haven't established rapport or relationship (personal or business) with this person. They may not know you well enough to trust you or know what kind of person you may be. So, they may not know how to support you in your quest. Be mindful that people are fickle. Not every person in your network is someone you should be asking for a referral. Be selective, be intentional and see how things go.

Be comfortable and confident in your request

Do not forget to sound and act natural when asking for referrals. You don't have to use a script, and it can be very informal. Test what works best for you. The most important thing is that you feel comfortable asking; otherwise, you may find yourself asking less and less until you no longer ask at all.

Use more than one source
The Second Step

Getting a referral is only part of expanding your reach. You need to follow up with your network to make sure you get everything you need to turn that referral into a qualified lead.

The most basic necessity of a referral

One obvious and crucial part of turning that referral into a prospect is making sure you get the contact information from your referral source. It may take a few touches to motivate your referral source enough to give you the information you need to make contact and follow up.

Do not cold call referrals

Before you call your new prospect, however, you need to get your network to contact them first. This should not be a surprise unexpected cold call. Whether they call you or you call them, this connection should be planned, and they're looking forward to talking with you.

Everybody is not tall enough to ride the ride

Don't just get any referral from your network resources; make sure you get only quality referrals. You should have some guidelines that your referral source is aware of so they can set you up with only those people that are qualified. For example, the Divorce is final. They have their own place. They have a legal source of income, etc.

Quantify your potential gain

Make sure you can find the value of your referrals. When you speak with a potential prospect, I'll admit it's a bit of a fact-finding mission. Before you invest a lot of time and energy into this company, make sure you're asking the right questions. Obviously, you want to know a little about them to see if you have anything in common, but also after the icebreaker and easing your curiosity, ask the tough question, "How does your life work?" You want to know if this person even has time to date or invest in pursuing a relationship. Timing is especially important. Even if there's some attraction to that person, you want to uncover, through a series of conversations and/or dates, if you're compatible. When a business is in growth mode, one of the things to focus on are those revenue-generating activities. If what you're doing is not moving you closer to your goal, then you're going to learn boundaries and know when to say NO. If you discover that the person you're interacting with doesn't have a life that you can see yourself partnering with, establish clear boundaries within yourself ahead of time and use your words to communicate what you need, so you're not wasting your time or theirs on non-revenue-generating activities just to say you had a conversation or went on a date when you know this is not a good fit.

For example, I met a gentleman at one of my son's AAU tournaments in Florida one year. He was very persistent and cute. On our first date, I asked the question, "So, tell me, how does your life work?" He proceeded to share how he refereed every weekend, he was starting his PhD program in the fall, he was taking care of his dad who had early dementia and lived with him, and the absolute deal breaker for me, he wanted a family. I may have forgotten to mention I was menopausal and traveled for work 3 or 4 weeks per month. Can you see how this was not a good fit?

The Third Step

The third and final step is to optimize your referral system. Do not just set it and forget it. You need to tweak things as you move on so that you can get the best results from it.

Stick to it

One reason why companies fail to generate referrals is because they don't follow the system. With a relationship strategy, as in business, you must inspect what you expect. Spend some time monthly just looking at your life. Have you improved your situation or are you still complaining about the lack of good men? Have you evolved? Referrals are just one way to leverage your resources, not the only way. Check in with your people. Are you staying in touch? Are you following up? Are you asking, or have you given up? You need a new set of resources from which to obtain referrals. This is your life, and you deserve to have everything you want. So, inspect what you expect, Keep working on it and improve incrementally so that you can get more return for your time spent and above all else, HAVE FUN!

Continuously Tweak

Don't assume that just because you have a referral system it's operating at peak efficiency. Go back and make changes and test new things to get the most you possibly can out of it.

Chapter 3
MARKETING PLAN

This section provides details on your industry, the competitive landscape, your target market, and how you'll market your business to those potential partners.

For existing companies, if you have determined your company is worth reinvesting in, then observe market research from the vantage point of what's comfortable. What are some things you did as a couple before you got married or became exclusive? Are you still dating? Are you still looking and feeling your best? I am an equal opportunity critic, so, if your partner has fallen off their game and it's impacting the relationship, it's time for a board meeting. What recommendations are you willing to make to support change? Don't complain about you never doing anything or going anywhere anymore; take ownership of this committee and plan date night, plan sex, plan an adult-only vacation, have a board meeting to discuss various issues and come up with some solutions. Life has a way of sneaking up on us, and we lose sight of the most important things that make life worth living.

I've never been a holiday or celebration type person. I just don't make a day a special day, I strive to live every day with a level of gratitude and appreciation. As humans, holidays are celebrated. It took my husband to bring to my attention that it's nice not to have the pressure of celebrating Valentine's Day or holidays when gifts are expected; however, some acknowledgement is nice like birthdays and anniversaries. Now, this didn't require a board meeting, but we did have a team meeting to discuss. This was important but not a big deal, just an observation. So, I stepped up my game when it comes to celebrations. I still think major holidays are over commercialized and all about money, but I meet my husband halfway in acknowledging milestones without going overboard.

Market research is an opportunity to observe the market, your environment and find ways to move out of the comfort zone.

Market Research

There are two kinds of research: *primary* and *secondary*. *Primary* market research is information you gather yourself. This would be taking inventory of your past relationships. Take the time to write down the pros and cons of each relationship or interaction, no matter how brief the encounter may have been.

Secondary market research is information from sources such as books, magazines, friends, families, extended families, colleagues, TV shows, reality TV, podcasts, scientific studies, etc. Any source outside of yourself is considered a secondary source. This is the section where you do your due diligence to work on self-improvement in health, money management, investing, real estate, whatever increases your market value…

This section of your plan should help to explain or better understand areas of opportunity for improvement in clarifying what you want:

- Trends in the industry: Do you have a type? When you look at past relationships, are certain characteristics consistent? For example, I only date men who are tall, physically fit, college graduate, rich, drive a certain kind of make/model, etc.
- The size of your target market: Where are you positioned to be found? Are you an introvert? Reclusive? Extremely social? Gym rat? Stay at home? Workaholic? Full-time parent? Lots of friends? No friends? Etc.
- Market share: What market share is realistic for you to obtain? What are you doing to expand your options? Hobbies, interests, trying something new, learning something new…

Barriers to Entry

What barriers exist mentally or physically that get in the way of lasting love? Barriers to entry might include:

- High startup costs – Unrealistic expectations?
- High production costs – Do you have income restrictions?
- High marketing costs – Do you have limiting beliefs around roles and responsibilities in a relationship?
- Brand recognition challenges
- Finding qualified employees – Do you have a reliable support system?
- Need for specialized technology or patents – Do you only date certain professions? Blue collar vs. white collar? Famous/Celebrity? Owner vs. Employee? Do you require or want someone with a specific background that can relate to your lifestyle?
- Liabilities – Do you suffer from Post-Traumatic Stress Disorder (PTSD)? This could be childhood trauma, sexual abuse, verbal abuse, panic attacks, any psychological reaction occurring after experiencing a highly stressing event that's usually characterized by depression, anxiety, flashbacks, recurrent nightmares, and/or avoidance of reminders of the event. These experiences may be relevant in terms of full disclosure, because if the residue is still affecting

areas of your life, your safety, your ability to experience intimacy, then you must give your potential life partner the opportunity to choose what they can and cannot handle.

Threats

Once your business surmounts the barriers to entry mentioned above and others that weren't mentioned, what additional threats might your company face? You cannot get to intimacy without going through vulnerability. Is there any residue that could still threaten the ability to merge your company with another company?

1. Fear
2. Jealousy
3. Unhealed wounds
4. Insecurity
5. Past trauma
6. Self-sabotage
7. Negative attitude
8. Control issues
9. Influential people in your life

Product/Services

Features and Benefits

What do you bring to the table? List each one. What value do these products and/or services add to your potential partner or partnership overall? If there are any life events that may alter the trajectory of a partnership, talking about it now can prevent it from becoming an issue later.

In this section, explain any after-sale services that you think are important to consider, such as:
- Children
- Elderly parents
- Retirement
- Change in career
- Loss of job/downsizing
- Health
- Relocation
- Purchase of a new home
- Refund policy – Prenuptial Agreement
- Life Insurance
- Life Planning

This section is designed to help you think through life events that may be more relevant for you than for others depending on your age. Gen Xers were born between 1965 and 1980, Baby Boomers I between 1946 and 1954, and Baby Boomers II between 1955 and 1964. These age groups may be taking care of elderly parents, raising grandchildren, downsizing, nearing retirement or retired, dealing with health issues, etc. Regardless of age, it's also important to discuss expectations within the roles and responsibilities that will be fulfilled. These are necessary issues to be discussed.

***To the Silent Generation, born between 1928 to 1945. Love can last forever at any age. The value of this generation, although the most susceptible physically to changes in the environment, is that they are also the most resilient, as extended history has shown their ability to navigate adversity.

If you are an existing corporation, have any of these issues affected your company? Have you had a board meeting to discuss what the next steps are? For example, if one of you is facing a health issue (e.g., COVID-19, mental health issues, a life-threatening medical issue etc.), this may affect the company financially as well as physically, emotionally, and mentally. Expected or unexpected, what's the strategy moving forward, and how do you ensure the company will continue to thrive? Do you need to hire help? Do one of you or your partner need to take on more responsibility in an area to pick up the slack for a little while? Whatever curve ball life throws at you, united you must stand and that starts with a plan.

Key Competitors

One of the biggest mistakes you can make in a business plan is to claim you have "no competition." Every business has competitors.

Your plan must show that you have identified yours and understand how to differentiate your business. What this means in your relationship strategy is that we can often be our own worst enemy. This is the time to be honest with yourself. What don't you like about yourself physically, mentally, financially, and socially? Are you an introvert, extrovert, have lots of friends, not enough friends, socially awkward, insecure, shy, low self-esteem? Only you know what lies behind the shadows, hidden in the dark. You can wear a mask in public, but to never take it off behind closed doors brings about a destruction to your Soul. If you aren't honest with yourself, then who can you be honest with? You cannot change what you're unwilling to acknowledge. What do you need to do to feel better about yourself?

Jealousy, envy, low self-esteem, the need of validation from your mate or anyone who will give you some attention, likes on your social media page, followers, etc. These are just a few of the underlying seeds that destroy partnerships. Can you imagine being in a relationship where you're always on? What are you afraid of that, if they knew, would change how they feel about you? Or is that what you tell yourself, so you don't have to deal with the person in the mirror?

Unforgiveness

Do you know nonforgiveness causes heart attacks and strokes? It clogs your arteries and eats away at your Soul. It creates blockages that prevent the blood from flowing freely through your veins, and it attacks the flow of blood to the heart. Forgiveness releases pain that keeps you trapped in a vicious cycle of negativity (poison). Nonforgiveness is like venom that slowly seeps into your bloodstream and becomes so toxic that it kills the host (the one who holds onto the poison). Nonforgiveness has no negligible effect on the person(s) you're unwilling to forgive. Making a conscious, deliberate decision to release feelings of resentment or vengeance toward a person or group who has harmed you, regardless of whether they deserve your forgiveness, releases you from the recurrent pain that you inflict upon yourself every time you recite what was done to you.

Take back your power. Gratitude is a powerful sword to defeat darkness and promote healing. In positive psychology research, gratitude is strongly and consistently associated with greater happiness. Gratitude helps people feel more positive emotions, relish good experiences, improve health, deal with adversity, and build strong relationships.

In business, there's a noun in the stock market called an Initial Public Offering (IPO). Going through this process is not about selling pieces of yourself to the highest bidder who can afford to invest and own a piece of you, but the analogy from a common language perspective is simply to imply that you're doing the work on self to present your best, highest expression of yourself to the world and to declare that you're open and ready to receive whatever you say and believe from all the goodness and abundance the Universe has in store for you, including your life partner. And you will receive it all in perfect divine timing. It is the Law of Assumption.

Chapter 4
OPERATIONAL PLAN

This section explains the daily operation of your business and processes.

Quality Control

How will you maintain consistency? What are your accountability markers? Describe the quality control procedures you will use. When you've spent a lot of time thinking about your ideal mate, dreaming, fantasizing, visualizing what it's like having them as a part of your life, it's normal to be sucker punched by your outdated programming, the voice of reason as it pertains to your logical mind, your physical reality that feels so real it's almost impossible to ignore. If you look around and there are no prospects in your vicinity, then you begin to ask yourself, a reasonably intelligent, educated, and successful person, if you're really falling for this scam. What were you thinking? Did you really believe all you had to do was imagine a man/woman who adores you, respects you, doesn't need you, but wants you and wants to build a future with you? Did you really think that was all it was going to take?

Now, you are starting to question everything. Quality control says, when you imagine this relationship, your heart opens. You feel so loved and appreciated. Your life has even more meaning because your light uplifts others, and you have the capacity to do more, be more. So, the love of your life is not physically with you, but they are with you. And knowing that keeps you full. Everything in your life is better with or without the physical manifestation. When you get there, it is inevitable. The purpose of the plan is to identify and define what you want in a relationship. Having it or not having it doesn't stop you from living a full, robust, joyous life. Not having the relationship made you sad, but having the experience without needing the physical manifestation is the secret.

Second guessing yourself is no longer an option. Everything you need you already have. As you lean into that knowing, everything you could imagine is yours. From this space, tell your story.

Quality control is being mindful of those thoughts that may creep into your mind triggered by the happiness of others. This is not to say you're not happy for other people who've found love and feel you're equally deserving, but it can be a reminder of what you don't have. Feelings are not right or wrong; they just are. What can be incredibly challenging is living in and experiencing the joy of your imagination while being faced with the reality that the person isn't physically there. Having some strategies in place before this happens gives you the best chance of success to weather those human moments and not lose hope or faith that your desire will happen.

Will it be reasonable to expect that when you become more conscious, more intentional, people will start showing up in your experience from your past? Yes. Random individuals? Yes. Now that you're being more mindful of what you're focusing on, when you start paying attention, all kinds of things will start showing up. It's referred to as all hell breaking loose. You still must live life. Now, you can choose to go into hibernation because you know you're not ready for the responsibility, the demands of being in a relationship, or you can try to date while healing. When people are showing up, the clearer you are about what you desire, the easier it will be not to get distracted or caught up in the game. It may be tempting, but if you've made your list, and the individual you're dealing with is already displaying red flags, don't pass go, don't collect $200. Abort the mission and get the hell out of this situation immediately. Debrief – what was I thinking? Thoughts of fear and what I don't want to happen or what I am trying to prevent from happening… I know it will feel like it's the other person, but it's not, it's always you. And it could be as simple as recognizing a time when you would have stayed and given this person multiple chances than they deserved but you decided quicker that this was not what you want, and you pivot. Either way, you can measure growth or the lack thereof.

That's what it means to live on purpose. What you think about, you bring about. I want to also let you know that once you have decided what you want, you can still have it without a lot of attention to it. Sounds like a contradiction, doesn't it? When you have developed enough faith in the law, you can make the declaration that what you want has happened and without worrying about it or measuring how long it may be taking, your belief is unwavering. That takes practice to get to that point. Some things are easier than others to not focus on, but gauge how you feel. If thinking about what you want hurts, that's the indication that you've gone far enough. Shut it down for now. Only focus on what you want for as long as you want if it feels good. When you start getting anxious, afraid, worried, overwhelmed, that's your signal that enough is enough for now. When your imagined experience is no longer pleasing, then it's time to take a break. Just for a little while. Live to dream another day.

What are some things you can do to manage the gap while you're in the chrysalis stage? Find things in your life for which you're grateful. Go beyond the surface, Ask yourself what storm did I survive? What obstacle have I overcome that built strength? What do I know now that I didn't know then that serves me well? Gratitude is more than what you see. Gratitude destroys all doubt, fear, and unbelief. I promise you; your heart opens and overflows when you remind yourself of how blessed you are.

Encourage yourself. Remind yourself that you're loved, appreciated, and worthy of unconditional love, unending joy, and happiness. You deserve to share your life with someone who loves, respects, adores, and appreciates you. Fully understand the power of your emotions and their impact. Your subconscious mind, the seat of your emotions, emanates a vibration. If the vibration is high, you attract good things into your life, but when your vibration is low, you attract not so good things into your life. Abraham Hicks created an Emotional Guidance Scale, so when those negative thoughts come, and they will, depending upon how long you entertain them, they will be manifested in how you feel. Connecting the thought with the feeling will help you understand the cause and then practice how to use the Emotional Guidance Scale, another tool in your toolbox.

Here's the scale of emotions from highest to lowest. These emotions are emotions that are conducive to attracting positive outcomes and manifesting your desires, (Foster, 2021)…

1. Joy/Appreciation/Empowerment/Freedom/Love
2. Passion
3. Enthusiasm/Eagerness/Happiness
4. Positive Expectation/Belief
5. Optimism
6. Hopefulness
7. Contentment
8. Boredom
9. Pessimism
10. Frustration/Irritation/Impatience
11. Overwhelm (feeling overwhelmed)

12. Disappointment
13. Doubt
14. Worry
15. Blame
16. Discouragement
17. Anger
18. Revenge
19. Hatred/Rage
20. Jealousy
21. Insecurity/Guilt/Unworthiness
22. Fear/Grief/Desperation/Despair/Powerlessness

So How Do We Use the Emotional Guidance Scale?

The Emotional Guidance Scale is laid out to help us identify where we are emotionally. If we're in a low place and want to feel better, it's important to first identify where we are on the scale and then give ourselves permission to climb the ladder and reach for a higher vibration. It's important to remember that it's impossible to jump to joy if you're in a state of feeling jealous, angry, or discouraged. As you're moving up the emotional scale, be easy about the timetable. I don't want you to spend one second longer in a negative emotion than you have to, yet some stages may take a little bit longer than others. Just keep reaching for a better feeling emotion and, gradually, you'll find hope. And If you can get to hope, you can begin to believe that things are working out for you. Two of the most powerful words in the Universe are Thank You. If you force a feeling of joy, it will feel inauthentic and false, and you won't be able to truly move. Movement from one position to another is based on your thoughts. Being positive is intentional.

Joy is the Ultimate State of Attraction

When we live in a state of joy, we attract what we desire. Think of it this way: we attract what we put out there. So, if we're living in a state of joy, we tend to attract happy people and positive experiences that match that vibration. However, if we're living in a state of jealousy, hatred, or anger, we'll attract people and experiences that match that negative vibration. Ultimately, we choose who and what we attract by where we allow ourselves to stay on the emotional scale.

Jim Rohn said, "You're the average of the five people you spend the most time with." The first major study on the breadth of social influence was conducted by Nicholas Christakis and James Fowler. While examining the data set from the Framingham Heart Study, one of the largest and longest running health studies ever, they realized that it covered more than just the heart health of the participants. As they began to probe with all sorts of demographic questions, including questions about family members and friends, they found the effects of family members and friends and even friends of friends have an effect. The implication is not just being deliberate about who you're spending most of your time with, but you need to be examining your entire network and its influence on your life (Burkus, 2018).

How to Move Up the Emotional Scale

Ways to move up the scale include simple shifts like…

1. Remind yourself that even one step up is an improvement. In one hour, you can move from anger to discouragement to doubt and disappointment quickly. This may not sound like progress but it feels better than helpless. Just know you can move up the scale quickly.
2. Spend more time doing practices like meditation, energy work, prayer, yoga, spending time in nature. Commit to at least 30 minutes per day.
3. Remember that growth is a process and that you'll have good and bad days. This doesn't mean you aren't moving in the right direction.
4. Change the people you're spending your time with. When you spend time with people who are living in a state of joy (or close to it) they will help lift you up and remind you where you want to be.
5. Start practicing gratitude and shifting your thoughts from "Why is this happening to me?" To "I am so grateful for the following things in my life…"
6. Serve others. When you start feeling like you're living far from joy, it helps to serve others. By doing something else and focusing on other people's needs, you take your energy and focus

away from what you're missing and put it toward helping someone else. This naturally increases your vibration and helps you see beyond yourself and your own life.

7. Have fun! Another great way to get out of a "funk" and living at a higher vibration is by doing something that brings you joy. If you're having a rough day and feel like you can't handle all the things, maybe it's time to turn on music and have a dance party with your children. Or maybe fun for you is reading a book outside on your patio or plugging into music and going for a walk. Whatever brings you happiness or excitement, do it!

Remember, you manifest things all day long, even when you're not aware of it. That is why terrible things happen to good people. Even when you're not creating on purpose, you can create out of the oblivious.

Chapter 5
MANAGEMENT & ORGANIZATION

This section should give readers an understanding of the people behind your business, their roles and responsibilities, and their impact and/or contribution on who you're becoming.

If you're in an existing relationship, are there outside influencers who are affecting the organization? I remember I had one or two people in my innermost circle whom I could trust with my pain. My mother and other close associates and family weren't a part of that inner circle. Why? Because family or close friends usually take your side and when the dust settles, they're still mad at your partner while you two have kissed and made up.

This doesn't define every mother/daughter relationship or refer to wise counsel. But if your girlfriend can't manage her relationship(s), then why are you soliciting advice from her? If she knew what to do, you birds of a feather would not be together.

Biographies

Briefly describe the most influential people in your life who have shaped your attitudes and belief system. How have they impacted you now and/or in the past? What about their journey was passed on to you consciously or through observation?

Are you someone who hates to be alone? I don't mean lonely; that's an emotional state of being. Alone is a physical state of being. Are you uncomfortable with silence? Do you need to keep busy all the time? Is sitting still uncomfortable? Can you remember a time when you didn't have a man in your life? What example did your mother demonstrate to you that you've unconsciously absorbed? I don't think I was traumatized, but while hanging out with my dad, he taught me unconsciously to not get attached to things or even people. For most of my adult life, I've had an expiration date of about 4 years. Relocating to another state or city was normal, which means I'm also a minimalist. I don't keep a lot of stuff because it makes it hard to pick up and move when I'm ready to go. My mother, on the other hand, knew how to grind, how to work hard. She helped raise her siblings, so she taught me how to take care of a family and a man. I don't recall my mother ever asking for help, and, subsequently, I've had to learn how to develop that skill. I suffered in silence for years because I didn't know how to ask for what I needed, and, even today, I struggle at times.

I didn't grow up with a lot of rules, but I did grow up around judgment and criticism. It wasn't directed at me, but even in that environment, as a child, I internalized so much stuff that I didn't even realize it because who I am was influenced by my environment. I don't have low self-esteem, but I'm extremely self-critical, a perfectionist at times with myself. I had to learn to give myself some grace and be easy about things. I don't take everything so seriously, which is probably why I laugh all the time. I only have two switches, on and off. So, finding balance or harmony can be a struggle. I share this with you to demonstrate that, as children, what we see and hear is absorbed in our subconscious mind. Remember, this is the seat of our emotions, the storehouse of our memories. Everything we've ever experienced is locked in our subconscious mind or even deeper, the unconscious mind. So, when you're reacting to situations and circumstances, especially in a negative, destructive way, it's because those unconscious triggers are being activated, and you don't even realize it's a problem until you react or overreact to something that can cause you or someone else harm.

You may think I'm way off base, but I'll encourage you to do a genogram. What I mean is just start with your mother or grandmother if you can at the top of the org chart on one side and your grandfather at the top on the other side. Begin to trace their relationship journey to see if there's a pattern that appears in terms of the kinds of relationships they had, divorce, remarriage, violent or dysfunctional relationships, cheating, children outside the marriage or committed relationship, etc. As you map out these journeys, does it look like or sound like behaviors you're repeating in your relationships? Who we are is a collection of what we've experienced throughout our life up until now. Who we become will be a direct result of the choices we make moving forward. Awareness is the beginning of change. It's hard to change something you're unwilling to acknowledge. Our biology, who we've been programmed to become, was downloaded to us all before the age of seven. When it comes to child development, it's been said that the most crucial milestones in a kid's life occur by the age of 7. In fact, the great Greek philosopher Aristotle once said, "Give me a child until he's 7 and I'll show you the man."

Advisors

List the members of your advisory support team, including:

    a. Mother/Father/Sibling
    b. Best Friend
    c. Relative
    d. Coworker
    e. Colleague
    f. Consultants
    g. Therapist
    h. Mentors and other advisors

If they have experience or specializations that will increase your chances of success, explain. It's probably better to seek advice from those who have done or are doing what you want to do as opposed to someone who hasn't. You can't give me advice about making money if you're broke. You can't give me advice on how to be fit if you're not healthy? Perhaps being an example of what not to do can be of tremendous value.

If you're the smartest person in your circle, then you need a new circle. I needed to grow, but I worked from home, no social life, just existing inside my bubble. So, I asked the Universe to help me find a circle that I could grow in, stretch, and go to the next level. The Universe, in all its infinite wisdom, led me to an organization where all the genius creators reside. I had access to knowledge like Scale Your Business to $1M when I wanted to grow my business to 1 million dollars, Mastering Authentic Networking, The Immunity Blueprint, Quantum Jumping, Be Extraordinary, Super brain, 10X, just limitless opportunities to access the knowledge that these incredible individuals possess to enhance my growth and spirituality. So, I didn't expand my circle in the traditional way, but being able to engage with others of like mind as I took these courses was life changing. If you're like me and don't know how to break the cycle, ask the Universe, Source Energy, or whatever you call God, and know that the answer will come.

After reading the Management & Organization section, you should feel confident that you have a qualified team supporting the Business of You.

Chapter 6

Financial Plan

Your financial plan is the most principal element of your business plan. Developing your financial plan helps you set financial goals for your business and assess its financing needs. If you have a sound financial portfolio, are there things that you could learn to enhance your profitability like cryptocurrency or digital real estate? Can you reinvest in a young person, a cause, the community? Money has no value if it's not working.

Let's put finances into perspective as it relates to a partnership. The top five reasons for divorce are (1) ***Adultery,*** (2) ***Money and finances,*** (3) ***Communication issues,*** (4) ***Addiction,*** and (5) ***"Simply falling out of love/no obvious problems."***

Money and finances are hot buttons for couples. Money arguments are the result of many things, such as different spending habits and financial goals. According to Dave Ramsey, money is the number one issue couples fight about or, worse, avoid discussing altogether, which leads to even more problems like communication issues. Understanding your relationship to money is as equally important as understanding the money management behaviors of a future partner. These five questions are for amateurs, but good to check in with, nevertheless.

Are you financially healthy? In research from GOBankingRates (2022), ask yourself these five questions to find out:

1. Are you making payments for fixed monthly expenses, such as rent and utilities, on time? Skipping payments or making payments late can affect your financial health for the worse. Missed fixed monthly payments can also be reported to credit bureaus and negatively impact your credit score.

2. Are you accumulating more credit card debt than you can pay off on time? "Mounting credit card debt can become a massive roadblock to financial stability," Lisa Fischer, chief lending, and growth officer at Mission Lane, said. "An accumulation of credit card debt is a more urgent concern now than ever as inflation is driving product prices up and causing many individuals to burn through their savings more quickly than anticipated. This may leave individuals with even less left each month to pay off existing debt, and in turn, this debt will

continue to increase as interest is added each month."

There is a strategy that may be useful. If you cannot tackle your most expensive credit card first, then take the credit card you owe the least amount on. Double the payment while maintaining the minimum balance due on the other credit cards. What you're seeking to accomplish is maintain on time payments on your existing credit cards and begin paying off the other credit card by doubling the amount due. Each month that balance should go down. Once you've paid that off in less time because you're doubling up on the payments, take that money and add it to the next credit card with the least amount owed. Same principle, divide and conquer. Instead of paying the minimum amount due, you are doubling and then some what you normally pay. This will reduce the principle and therefore the amount of interest you're paying monthly. If you can make an extra payment per month, you could pay what's due for on-time payments. Then make another payment with the extra toward the principle only. This way you're tackling the principle which lowers the amount of interest being paid. Another strategy if possible is to split the payment in half and instead of paying the bill one time per month, pay half on the 1st of the month and the other half on the 15th. This strategy again pays down the principle and reduces the interest being paid on the balance.

3. **Are you prioritizing spending on essentials, such as food and healthcare, rather than entertainment and other nonessentials?**

Look at exactly where your money is going and what categories you're spending the most on. Ideally, you'll be spending more on needs than wants. If you follow the 50/30/20 rule, for example, 50% of your income should be dedicated to essentials, such as housing, transportation, and groceries; 30% can go toward wants or discretionary spending; and 20% should be dedicated to savings. Create a simple budget or use a budget tracker app to help you manage your spending and differentiate your wants from your needs.

4. **Are you able to save a portion of your monthly income for emergency funds?** Many people still have no savings or extraordinarily little: Nearly one in five Americans didn't save any money in 2021, according to recent data from the latest Magnify Money Savings Index. And 18% of respondents admittedly contributed zero dollars to their savings last year, and another 48% contributed fewer than $5,000. Bankrate's July 2021 Emergency Savings <u>survey</u> revealed that a quarter of Americans have no emergency fund at all and just one in six households report having more savings now than prior to the pandemic.

5. **Do you have Long-Term Savings?** "In addition to having savings for an emergency fund,

individuals should ask themselves if they have sufficient long-term savings," Fischer said. "Whenever you can, it's advantageous to set aside money for retirement, education or other longer-term goals. In general, the more you focus on your financial health in your early years, the more comfortably you can live in your later years."

If you're feeling far behind about your savings, be patient. Pros say you should start small. Do not expect to pile up savings overnight. It may take many years of diligent saving to get to the point where your emergency cushion is built up to manage six months of expenses and you're ready to focus on saving for longer-term goals like retirement or your kids' college funds, according to Greg McBride, chief financial analyst at Bankrate.com.

One big no-no when it comes to savings is putting it in an account that pays little (the average savings account is only paying 0.06% now). But accounts with higher APYs ("annual percentage yield" which is a number that indicates how much interest a bank account, such as a certificate of deposit, earns in one year) do exist. The bottom line is you must start somewhere, even if all you can set aside is the $5 to open a savings account. If you have a savings account, pay attention to it. Shop around. Remember, start!

If you are looking for ways to invest to build wealth that lasts, here are some options to consider:

- Stock ETFs and mutual funds
- Low-cost index funds
- Real estate, or REITs
- Money market funds
- Online savings accounts
- Treasury Bills
- Certificates of Deposit

***Please seek the advice of a certified financial advisor for more information.

Fiscal responsibility is a mindset that a potential company can build and grow with. Being honest with yourself and taking action to improve your financial acuity will allow you to be more transparent and secure when it comes to finances. If your partner is better at managing money, that does not mean you give up having a say or influence as to how the money is being spent, there is no" I" in TEAM. If the electric bill doesn't get paid, when they turn the lights off, you're both in the dark. Identify your belief system about money.

When you're contemplating a merger, go through this process to ensure you're having open, honest dialog about how each of you run your business, and if you're contemplating a merger, this is the due diligence that's required before you sign legal documents. Full transparency. This is the time to have the hard conversations. Finding out that the business is not profitable after the merger creates additional stressors on the relationship, inhibiting growth as you try to move forward.

Regardless of your net worth, having the conversation about money is good business. If that results in a prenuptial agreement, remember this is business not personal. What you two build together is personal. I am not an advocate for or against. I am a champion for the necessity to have the conversations that matter, that if you avoid them or make unsubstantiated assumptions based on what you think and not what you know, this will be considered an act of aggression and will be a threat to the long-term stability of the organization.

Operations

Credit Policies

Do you know your credit score? Are you positioned to build or expand your company based on your current credit score? When you talk about the growth of a company through a merger, both partners are responsible for the ability to expand. Using other people's money is how wealthy people build more wealth. If you are not credit worthy through irresponsibility, these conversations must take place before the merger or acquisition of future assets. Maybe poor credit is a result of downsizing, bad investments, the economy. No matter the reason, full disclosure must be given. You must give your potential partner the opportunity to decide how they want to move forward with their company since those types of decisions moving forward will impact their company as well.

This conversation is food for thought for you in that you have been managing your company all these years alone. What are your expectations when it comes to the merger? Will you continue to manage the financial aspects of the company separately or jointly? Will certain aspects of the company be merged, or will they continue to operate independently? Is there any part of the finances to manage jointly? These are partnership conversations.

If you are in an existing corporation and the company is suffering both financially and emotionally, have you had a board meeting to discuss the issues. Agree upon a day and time, create an agenda, if you have suggestions, bring them to the meeting, and, remember, if the company is in trouble and at risk of shutting down, as the CEO, you must have the hard conversations. Suffering in silence has never been a method for success. Be open and honest. Even if you don't know what to do, like any strategy session, work together to brainstorm, share ideas, keep talking. If you're at an impasse, bring in a third party. Do whatever it takes to bring about a peaceful resolution. If new agreements are made and not followed, only you know when enough is enough and it's time to take drastic action. This breakdown in communication didn't happen overnight, and a resolution may not happen overnight. When you go through arbitration, it takes time. If, ultimately, the corporation cannot be saved, stand tall and know that you've done everything you know to do to fix the situation, but it takes two. And remember, not all companies are successful, and reconciling that within yourself is sometimes good enough.

After reading the Operational Plan section, you should understand how your business will operate daily. What are your goals and strategies for growth in the future?

Break-even Calculation

The break-even analysis projects the sales volume you need to cover your costs in business like your rent, utilities, salaries that aren't revenue generating but paid every month, etc. In a relationship, let's define break-even as your nonnegotiable. Instead of looking at what you must sell each month or each year to cover the cost of doing business, let's apply this strategy to understanding what factors can threaten your company when you're out of alignment.

What's your potential partner's credit score? Do they pay their bills on-time? What is their relationship with money? What is their belief system about money? How have they managed their company? How they manage their company is a good indicator of what their financial behavior will be like jointly. If there are concerns going into the merger, get alignment and prenuptial agreements, if necessary, prior to closing the deal.

In many situations, when a company goes through a merger, risks need to be assessed. If child support is a liability for one of the partners, how will that affect the revenue that's generated after the merger? What about student loan debt, children, college, looking after an elderly parent, future investments such as buying a new home together and selling or renting the other property? Will these additional expenses be shared or continue to be covered by the owner? These are conversations that need to be explored, if they apply, prior to signing the contract.

A Break-even can also be defined when something is a recurring pattern of behavior that threatens the overall stability of the relationship and, after several conversations, there has been no demonstrated change in behavior, then it may be time to consider professional help or pivot and move in a different direction.

The reason there's so much chaos and drama in relationships is because people are not honest and are unwilling to set boundaries out of fear that if they don't do something, someone else will. Now, you are part of the problem. You may believe there are external competitors, and some people deflect to not wanting to put a label on the relationship. I get it, it feels like things change when you start labeling things. Well, what label do you call two people who are married? I haven't experienced being in a committed and/or exclusive relationship unknown. If you're in a relationship, you're in a relationship. What about that situation you don't want others to know about? I'm not looking to invite any unnecessary drama into my life. If that's an issue, I would call it a red flag. If your image conflicts with your revenue, then your actions still need to be consistent with your commitment. Again, these are conversations that a partnership requires.

I remember dating a guy whom I really liked, but he was still grinding to get established. One of his potential opportunities was to be in a pilot like *The Bachelor*. Really? And how do you think something like that would affect the relationship? I took the initiative and canceled any further episodes. I wasn't interested in being his secret so he could elevate his career. The partner who's divinely set aside for you isn't looking for any co-stars when they have a leading lady.

Benjamin Franklin said, "Honesty is the best policy." Chaos ensues when one or both parties aren't honest about what they want in a relationship. If you want to be married, then don't invest your time in someone who doesn't want to get married. If you want children and the person you may be interested in doesn't want children, that's a bad investment. If a person doesn't want to be in a committed relationship, they prefer casual so they can see other people, have fun, and focus on their career or building their business; believe them. If people show you who they are and you don't believe them, that's on you.

If you haven't invested the time and energy to develop your relationship business plan, you'll spend a lot of time pursuing bad investments. If you find yourself in one unhealthy relationship after the other, take heed. Why are you attracting all these companies that look good on the outside but have no furniture on the inside? The lights are off, no support system, broke at an elevated level, credit score jacked up, they have no assets in their name, they leverage your knowledge, financial resources, and connections to get ahead. How is that benefiting you? Pay attention!

Let us take it a step further. What if they're on the same playing field, but they're playing a different game? You are not a priority, ever. You accommodate them all the time, what's convenient for them. They don't take in consideration what's going on in your life as long as you make yourself available for them. Do they text rather than call? When you call, do they ever call you back soon, not days or weeks later? Is vulnerability a trigger? Every time you start having those real conversations, do they pop off, avoid, deflect? When there is a disagreement, do they shut down, withdraw, ignore you for days, even if you're in the same space? What 6-year-old are you considering partnering with to build your empire?

Nothing changes until you change. Another company cannot give you courage. Courage is the opposite of conformity. Another company is not supposed to be where you get your self-esteem, determine your worth or value, affirm or validate who you are. If that's how you measure your success, then you'll always be at the mercy of some force, condition, or situation outside yourself that you cannot control. This will guarantee you a seat on the emotional rollercoaster ride of life, and you'll be unstable in all your ways.

What are your top three non-negotiables? These are things that you're unwilling to tolerate under any circumstances. Even if you can forgive, the relationship becomes irreparable. The legal system calls them irreconcilable differences. These are conversations that should be discussed in the

G&D phase of the relationship. Live, Love, Laugh, and pay attention!

EMOTIONAL CURRENCY

What's Mental Health?

Mental health includes our emotional, psychological, and social well-being. It affects how we think, feel, and act. It also helps determine how we handle stress, relate to others, and make healthy choices, ("Mental Health: Strengthening Our Response," 2022). Mental health is important at every stage of life, from childhood and adolescence through adulthood. Although the terms are often used interchangeably, poor mental health and mental illness are not the same.

Why is Mental Health important for overall health?

Mental and physical health are equally important components of overall health. For example, depression increases the risk for many types of physical health problems, particularly long-lasting conditions like diabetes, heart disease, and stroke ("Diabetes and Mental Health," 2022). Similarly, the presence of chronic conditions can increase the risk for mental illness.

Can your Mental Health change over time?

Yes, it's important to remember that a person's mental health can change over time, depending on many factors. When the demands placed on a person exceed their resources and coping abilities, their mental health could be impacted. For example, if someone is working long hours, caring for a relative, or experiencing economic hardship, they may experience poor mental health.

1 in 5

How common are Mental Illnesses?

Mental illnesses are among the most common health conditions in the United States ("Mental Health: Strengthening Our Response," 2022).

- More than 50% will be diagnosed with a mental illness or disorder at some point in their lifetime.
- 1 in 5 Americans will experience a mental illness each year.
- 1 in 5 children, either currently or at some point during their life, have had a seriously debilitating mental illness.
- 1 in 25 Americans live with a serious mental illness, such as schizophrenia, bipolar disorder, or major depression.

What causes Mental Illness?

There's no single cause for mental illness. Several factors can contribute to risk for mental illness, such as

- Early adverse life experiences, such as trauma or a history of abuse (for example, child abuse, sexual assault, witnessing violence, etc.)
- Experiences related to other ongoing (chronic) medical conditions, such as cancer or diabetes
- Biological factors or chemical imbalances in the brain
- Use of alcohol or drugs
- Entertaining feelings of loneliness or isolation

Physical Health Currency

Ralph Waldo Emerson said, "The first wealth is health." Physical health is defined as **the condition of your body, taking into consideration everything from the absence of disease to fitness level**. Physical health is critical for overall well-being, and can be affected by lifestyle: diet, level of physical activity, and behavior (for instance, smoking); Physical health includes our **endurance, strength, flexibility, cardiovascular, digestive health,** and more. This is how prepared our body is each day to move through the world.

We do not seem to talk openly about having children. As women, we're born with all the eggs we'll ever have, about 2 million of them. By age 37, you'll have about 25,000 eggs left. By 51, you'll only have 1,000 eggs left. Not only do the number of eggs decrease but the quality of your eggs decreases with age also. If you have other risk factors like endometriosis and tubal disease, which increase with age, these conditions can negatively impact fertility. As you're climbing the proverbial corporate ladder to success, if children or a family is a possibility that you might want to consider at some point in time, I would encourage you to talk with your doctor as soon as possible to find out if freezing your eggs is an option. Choices. You want to always have the option.

For my more seasoned sisters, let's just briefly touch on menopause. Why is that topic needed? If you are entering into a partnership and are morphing into the Wicked Witch of the West, this affects your partner. This wasn't a subject covered in college in any course I took. Whether you're premenopausal, menopausal, or postmenopausal, it's like another stage in the evolution after you've gone from caterpillar to pupa, to a beautiful butterfly to Queen Bee, and if you live long enough, you'll be referred to as an "Empress." Men are ill-equipped to manage menopause. Although a natural and inevitable part of life, women are not having these conversations amongst ourselves.

I remember the pivotal moment when I entered menopause when I was 50 and I bled for 40 days straight. Thank God I was not in a relationship at that time. I thought I would die because there was no way a person could lose that much blood and still live. After that, there was nothing left. I was probably more equipped than most with insider information. As a pharmaceutical representative 14 years prior, I trained with a physician who was getting his certification in Bioidentical Hormones and taught a class in conjunction with one of my sponsored medical events. It was not covered by insurance then or now, but I knew I was not going to be one of those grouchy old women who always seemed to have an attitude, was bitter toward men, and had no desire for sex. No, ma'am, that was not going to be my future. I purposely had an HSA account for the sole purpose of being able to pay for this medical treatment when the time came. You must see a doctor who specializes in bioidentical hormones. The treatment is custom, and the level of investment is for life. I have energy, I sleep well, I maintain muscle mass, it stabilizes my mood, I'm not irritable or sluggish, and my sex drive and desire are at optimal levels. If you struggle with any of the symptoms listed below, I recommend you talk with your doctor and see someone who specializes in bioidentical hormones.

Symptoms

In the months or years leading up to menopause (perimenopause), you might experience these signs and symptoms:
- Irregular periods
- Vaginal dryness
- Hot flashes
- Chills
- Night sweats
- Sleep problems
- Mood changes
- Weight gain and slowed metabolism

- Thinning hair and dry skin
- Loss of breast fullness

Signs and symptoms, including changes in menstruation can vary among women. You will experience some irregularity in your periods before they end.

Skipping periods during perimenopause is common and expected. Often, menstrual periods will skip a month and return, or skip several months and then start monthly cycles again for a few months. Periods also tend to happen on shorter cycles, so they're closer together. Despite irregular periods, pregnancy is possible. If you have skipped a period but aren't sure you've started the menopausal transition, consider a pregnancy test.

When to See a Doctor

Keep up with regular visits with your doctor for preventive health care and any medical concerns. Continue getting these appointments during and after menopause.

Preventive health care as you age may include recommended health screening tests, such as colonoscopy, mammography, and triglyceride screening. Your doctor might recommend other tests and exams, too, including thyroid testing if suggested by your history, and breast and pelvic exams.

Always seek medical advice if you have bleeding from your vagina after menopause.

After reading the Financial Plan section, you should understand the assumptions behind your financial projections and other variables that may impact your ability to contribute to the financial stability of the company and be able to judge whether these projections are realistic. The value to your business reaches beyond the money. Your health and your peace of mind are more valuable than silver and gold.

Now That You are (Almost) Finished . . .

There's one more topic to discuss, and that's what options do you have if all else fails?

EXIT STRATEGY

An exit strategy is often thought of to end a business, which it can be, but in best practice, it's a plan that moves a business toward long-term goals and allows a smooth transition to a new phase, whether that involves reimagining business direction or leadership, keeping financially sustainable, or a strategic plan to sell his or her ownership in a company to another company.

There are several exit strategies a company has at their disposal, none of which should be taken lighly. For example, a merger, liquidation, or filing for bankruptcy. In the world of business, other strategic maneuvers one could consider would be an acquisition, an initial public offering (IPO), management buyout, or selling to someone you know. The Strategic Relationship Plan will focus on strategies to consider before the merger and a strategy forward after the merger.

- Estate Planning
- Be transparent about your finances (Social Security, Disability, Retirement, etc.)

- Consider the cost of long-term care
- Marriage penalty or marriage bonus?
- Dealing with debt
- Will
- Life Insurance

Communication is key. Unfortunately, second marriages have additional barriers that may be more challenging to navigate. Regardless of age or previous relationships, as you're building a life together, these should be topics of discussion to continue alignment as the relationship continues to evolve.

Merger

A merger is an agreement that unites two existing companies into one new company. The Strategic Relationship Plan is a blueprint designed to help individuals to know what they want. And sometimes, the process requires you to go through research and development to refine with precision what you want in your mate. Once you have gained clarity about what you want, you must go about the mission of imagining what that relationship looks like if you were already having that experience NOW. Not one day in the future, right now. The magic of the emotion infused within the imagination is what activates the subconscious to begin to move heaven and earth to manifest the desires of your heart.

I would love to offer you a lifetime warranty on your investment, but that's not possible. What is possible is the power that resides on the inside of you to always be the creator of your reality. If, for whatever reason, things don't go according to plan, having made peace with understanding, should anything happen, you have some comfort in knowing all is not lost.

The goal when you started this journey was to use a system, a method of attracting your ideal mate. If you're in an existing relationship and you're experiencing some turbulence, or you're at a crossroad needing some guidance, this process will create clarity, so you know the next step. Ultimately, the destination is to be in a healthy, loving, thriving relationship. If you're looking to go public and are ready for a merger, please use this blueprint to develop the new company to ensure you're equally yoked.

If you're in a relationship and it feels like things have changed, then reevaluate the relationship using the blueprint. Establish a Strategic Relationship Plan as a company under new management. What's the vision, mission, and purpose of the company? Who are you as a team? What is your purpose? If there's an opportunity to establish and realign your goals, then decide how that needs to happen. Look at the marketplace, the environment in which the company operates in and decide what your short- and long-term goals are. Are they aligned with where you want to go in the next year, 3 years, 5 years? Sometimes, things change. Be willing to negotiate or renegotiate the terms of the contract. What can WE do to save the company? What are WE willing to do? Forgive? Establish new goals? Set new boundaries? Seek counseling or therapy? Are the two of you fully committed to rebuilding the company? If yes, then decide how to move forward. If not, then consider liquidation.

Liquidation

Liquidation refers to the process of selling off a company's inventory or assets and is a precursor to a business closing. As painful as this option may be, if you've done all you know to do to save the company and you're continuing to be disappointed, let down, hurt by the decisions and choice of another, then you have two options. Like any thriving business, you may be faced with a scandal. You can pivot and move in a different direction to save your contribution to the company, or you can go down with the ship and lose everything. Either way, you cannot escape the pain or loss, but you can mitigate the damages by stepping away from the situation to gain a broader perspective. It's hard to see the picture when you're in the frame. The truth lies within you. Everything you want is on the other side of what you do not want, but it takes courage to confront the elephant in the room and even more courage to pursue happiness by any means necessary.

Bankruptcy

Although liquidation can be a part of a bankruptcy, let's go beyond the financial aspect of bankruptcy. Let's consider being emotionally, physically, and mentally bankrupt. Often, as women, we're programmed to give more than we get in return; sacrifice is noble. "Self-care is not an indulgence. It's a discipline" (Forman, 2019); it requires a tough-mindedness, a deep and personal understanding of your priorities and a respect for both you and the people you choose to spend your life with. For example:

- Choosing to binge watch another episode instead of going to bed so you can get up to go to the gym.
- Declining the second drink at the holiday party, or even the first drink.
- Saying "No" to the thing you don't want to do even if you know someone is going to be angry with you.
- Being fiscally responsible, financially independent.
- Letting other people take care of themselves.

It takes discipline, it takes practice to make decisions that are good for us, not just feel good in the moment. One of the greatest gifts we can give to ourselves is having the discipline to refuse to take responsibility for other people's emotional well-being. We tend to make self-care sound like an event when it's something we should practice daily. This approach keeps you from binging to restore balance. When you're truly practicing self-care, you're more equipped to show up in the world for yourself and for those you care about with meaning and purpose.

If restoration is beyond your ability to achieve at this point, after all viable options have been explored, and alignment cannot be achieved, create next steps to dissolve the relationship as amicably as possible. This path is never easy to navigate, so seek outside counsel, legally and emotionally as needed. Have a clear path forward, even if it's not a final plan. Remember, success is having a goal, and moving toward it.

Chapter 7
THE FINAL STEP
EXECUTIVE SUMMARY

"To desire is to obtain, to aspire is to achieve."
- James Allen

The Executive Summary is the most important part of your business plan. Often, it's the only part that a prospective investor or lender reads before deciding whether to read the rest of your plan. It should convey your enthusiasm for your business idea and get readers excited about it, too.

The same process applies for your Strategic Relationship Plan. This is a comprehensive overview of you, and if you choose to share it with a potential life partner, this blueprint can become the foundation upon which to build your legacy and provide transparency into both you and your potential life partner's companies to determine if this is a good fit.

The Executive Summary will be the first section and introduction to your Strategic Relationship Plan but it will be the very LAST section you write. That way, you'll have thought through all the elements of your startup or existing business and be prepared to summarize them.

This is a living breathing document that will continue to grow and change over time and needs to be revisited and revised as life continues to unfold. What's important to note, however, is that you're clear about what you want, and you can articulate it so vividly, that you begin to experience the effects of a healthy partnership before that partnership manifests into your reality.

After reading the Executive Summary, your potential partner should have a fundamental understanding of your business and should be excited about its potential and intrigued enough to read further.

Remember, the Executive Summary is a comprehensive overview of your Strategic Relationship Plan. Should the individual you share this with want to see what's behind the yellow tape, so to speak, the down and dirty of how you got to the clean and pretty overview, then they can read beyond the Executive Summary.

In the remainder of this chapter, I will give a more in-depth explanation of what is contained in an Executive Summary. The overall goal is to summarize the business of you into one or two pages. When you feel like you have a pretty good overview of the company, what it is and where it's going, you can summarize it in one to two pages. The Executive Summary is an overview of the company that highlights the main points of a larger report. Your strategy should establish who you are, what you (the company) stand for, and why you exist. Your strategy should define the company you have merged with and what impact you'll have on the world around you. You should be able to articulate in the plan where the merged company is going in a particular timeframe and how you propose to get there. I see the strategy as knowing who you are, what you want, where you're going, and how you plan to make that a reality. Remember, this is a document that's viable. It's updating as the things in your life are updating and expanding.

If you're not in a relationship now, that's mere commentary. The focus isn't where you are but where you'll be. All the work that's being asked of you is necessary to uncover what you really want. Many times, there's so much clutter, you can never see a way out. But the only way to get out is you have a burning desire to be out. So, tackling some of those demons that keep you bound is part of the work. You're more powerful than you think, and my hope is, even if we haven't conquered all your fears, you have the tools so that when you're ready, you know where to find them and how to use them. This is your work; this is your movie. You can rewrite the ending as many times as you want. The moral of the story is you win. And truly, a happy, fulfilling life is your birthright.

Practice doesn't make you perfect but it does allow for improvement. The more you improve your ability to Deconstruct Fear, the less time you spend in doubt and unbelief which is a form of mental and physical torture. Fear doesn't go away, but it is a tremendous indicator that it's time to go to the next level. Next level thinking, next level doing, next level being. Fear is challenging you to go higher. It can be a bully or your biggest motivator. Life is unpredictable and growth is uncomfortable. The tools you use and the skills you develop will serve you for eternity. Practice the exercises when you find yourself stuck or struggling to stay afloat, remember whatever the challenge, you win. Play the game of life as if it was rigged in your favor. Going through the process is just a formality, but I read the end of the book. You get what you believe. What do you believe?

Elements of an Executive Summary

The Executive Summary should briefly explain each of the topics below. If we were writing an actual business plan, this information would be relevant. However, our focus is on the business of you and finding your life partner; therefore, these elements will be modified and developed to craft a powerful executive summary of *From the Boardroom to the Bedroom: Her Heart. Her Hustle.*

1. **An overview of your business** idea (one or two sentences).

What this element is referring to is a brief description about you.

For example, I am a whole and complete being, lacking nothing, yet full of desires purposed to use my gift of teaching and speaking and inspiring others to greatness to serve the world and create immense wealth.

2. **A description of your product and/or service.**

What are your gifts and talents?

For example, I am a thinker. When I hear a problem, I often am figuring out a strategy to a solution. I can be task oriented. I like to get things done. I am a leader as well as a team player. I'll often solicit ideas from others, and ultimately will make the decision I feel is best for the company. I am not easily influenced and will do my own due diligence when it comes to making decisions that affect the company directly. Focus on your strengths, what you're good at.

3. **Your goals for the business.** Where do you expect the business to be in a year, 3 years, 5 years?

What this is asking you to do is think about (if you have not already done so), is where do you see yourself in the next 12 months, 2 and 3 years and can you articulate that? If that is too far ahead, start with bite-sized pieces: 3 months, then 6 months, then stretch into the next 12 months. This may be complex, and you may not have an answer for every area of your life but taking the time to contemplate where you would like to be or where you see yourself is important in getting to the destination. Wandering aimlessly through life, taking what life gives you, leads to an emotional rollercoaster ride. You'll always be the passenger instead of the driver of your life if you're not choosing where you want to go.

4. **Your proposed target markets.**

Target market is corporate lingo; however, giving some thought as to where you could position yourself to be found is worth thinking about. For example, if you want a mate who is fit and healthy, enjoys working out, then where would you expect to find someone with that lifestyle or interests? If being physically fit and being mindful of what you put in your body is important to you, not him, then intentionally get involved in events that support you and join clubs and gyms that are active. Explore and venture out. The value in this type of attitude is that you are doing something that's important to you. Should you meet someone along the way who has the same interests, then the joy and ability to sustain an activity is authentic. If you're doing things for other people, it won't last, and neither will the relationship because it's not founded on who you are, but the motive is based on what you can get out of it.

Listen to me carefully. When you do what satisfies your soul, it's not hard to sustain it and you reap the benefits. How many times have you done things to please other people only to end up resenting them later? If you're overweight and allergic to the gym and have zero desire to jog, walk fast, or eat a salad without dressing, then don't do it. If you feel guilty or have any negative emotion about not doing what others want you to do, I suggest you explore that feeling a little more to deconstruct what's really triggering those negative emotions.

What is the root cause of the fear and anxiety? You must make peace with your demons and let them go. The reason they still have power is because they thrive in the shadows. You have built a wall of protection around the pain to prevent anything from accidentally bumping up against them.

So, you've learned to live with the pain as opposed to healing the wound. Fear can be a bully or it can be your friend.

5. What are your Core Values? Here are a few examples, but feel free to add your own or select from the list:

- Loyalty
- Spirituality
- Humility
- Compassion
- Honesty
- Kindness
- Integrity
- Determination
- Generosity
- Courage
- Tolerance
- Trustworthiness
- Equanimity
- Altruism
- Empathy
- Toughness
- Self-Reliance
- Attentiveness

*** "There is a difference between the things you value and your actual values. The former come and go. But your values can guide you throughout your life, no matter the situation. In the end, you have a better measuring stick: real failure is failing to live by your values, and real success is acting every day to embody them." (Eyal, 2021)

6. **Your competition and what differentiates your business.** You're the biggest threat to the relationship plan. What programs are you consciously or unconsciously running that can sabotage your relationship?

We are often our biggest enemy. Let's start with taking a moment to reflect on our most impactful intimate relationships. Write down all the things that were good about those relationships in a notebook or a journal.

What I liked in my previous relationships…

What I did not like in my previous relationships… For example: He was not good with money. His priorities were fucked up!

On the third page, write: I want a partner who is fiscally responsible. I want a partner who respects and appreciates money. Go through, line by line, all the things you didn't like in each of those relationships until you have identified what you want in a partnership. This critical element is an important building block to the foundation of the boardroom.

Take what you did not like and reframe the statement.…

7. Your management team and their prior experience.

No person is an island. Whom would you consider your support system? Whom can you trust? I believe if you do not have at least one person on this earth who knows who you are and loves you anyway, then you must get to the business of building your tribe. Is life worth living if you have no one to share it with? A pet may be an incredible companion, but the last time I checked, their ability to exchange ideas and share experiences could be challenging. Not arguing the emotional support they can provide, just the logical or mental engagement that's valuable also.

The people in your corner, what do their lives look like? Birds of a feather flock together. Have you ever noticed how broke people want to give you advice on money? Why are single people giving advice about dating? Do not take relationship advice from people who don't know how to be in a healthy relationship, unless you're learning from their mistakes. My personal trainer cannot be fat. I go to a barber, but when I used to go to the salon, my stylist had to keep her wig tight.

Food for thought: Money doesn't hang out with broke people. Even money has standards.

8. Financial outlook for the business.

What has been your relationship with money? What unconscious agreements lay dormant when it comes to money? What was a running theme in your home about money? We cannot afford it. Money does not grow on trees.

Knowing your style of how you engage and interact with money is important.

Understanding your relationship with money is so important because partnership requires agreement on core issues. If you're a shopper and he's a saver, you don't have to change but you do have to compromise, work together. Letting one person take the lead on something like finances doesn't mean you don't have a say on how money is spent or invested. Partnership is not control over the other person ever in any area. Partnership is transparency, collaboration, and alignment between people who have nothing to hide. If you feel that because you may be the breadwinner, you can emasculate your partner, then Legacy Ownership (an individual who is self-sufficient, independent, and doesn't need to be in a committed relationship) may be something to consider. I'm not implying that you didn't work hard to get where you are, and I'm not suggesting you turn over the keys to the kingdom on everything you've built. What I am saying is from a business perspective, with legal counsel, protect your assets as well as he should, and if you two want to build a life together, what that looks like should be thoroughly discussed before the companies' merge.

Limit your Executive Summary to one or two pages in total. The above content is to ensure you've covered the major topics to consider in your relationship plan and the space to bring all the elements together while developing a strong foundation for a merger.

The definitive version of the Executive Summary will be rewritten and summarized in one or two pages in your *Journal*.

THE STRATEGIC RELATIONSHIP PLAN

CONGRATULATIONS!

There may still need to be some fine tuning as you continue to develop your strategy. Even if your relationship plan is not ready to present to a potential investor/partner, just giving thought to where you are currently in your life, what you really want, and what that looks like already gives you hope. It is no longer an idea or thoughts that come and go; it's intentional thinking with form to create strategy and direction. Now you move on purpose, not just by habit.

As we come to the end of this journey, I have included the 10 habits of successful relationships. Whether in the boardroom or the bedroom, having a goal and moving toward it is what success looks like. The mistake we as leaders often make is not knowing how to turn it off. A great leader's power is having the tools and knowing when to use them. You would never use a sledge hammer to bang a nail into a wall to hang a picture, and yet we do this in relationships all the time. We open our own doors, we reach for the check, we make all the decisions, solve all the problems, and forget to be receivers. Men love femininity cloaked in masculinity. He is not looking to compete in the boardroom and come home and compete in the bedroom. You can embrace all that makes you a woman without divorcing masculinity, you just have to know what super power to use at a specific time. I'm not asking you to give up anything, but just like any talent, you have to practice it to become really good at it. Don't give up and don't quit on me now, you got this. You just need to decide what you want and develop a plan and implement a strategy to live in your future, now.

I applaud you, my sister. I cannot wait to hear your testimony. Because you were willing to walk into the deep, not knowing what you might find, I believe if you continue to live in your future, your partner is waiting for you. And if it is the partner you already have, you've either given nourishment to provide the perfect environment for growth and expansion or, as a business owner, you've decided to downsize or close your business for renovations. This is an exciting time whatever your path. You're more equipped now than ever before to be the captain of your ship. Rise, for you have come for such a time as this. What are you waiting for? JUMP!

I have spent a lot of time talking about how your mind works and how to manage your emotions when manifesting your desires. One way to impress upon the subconscious what you desire is through repetition or habit. A habit is a routine of behavior that is repeated regularly and tends to occur subconsciously. The American Journal of Psychology defines a "habit, more or less as a fixed way of thinking, willing, or feeling acquired through previous repetition of a mental experience". According to Practical Psychology, 2022, here are ten habits for great relationships:

- Respect
- Communication
- Forgiveness
- Understanding
- Understanding what makes your mate feel loved
- Appreciating each other
- Focusing on the actual problem, not the conflict
- Knowing honesty comes first
- Being available for each other
- Laughing a lot

Bottom line: Cultivating positive habits takes no more effort than developing bad ones. When you start being honest with yourself about what you desire, and have a keen sense of self, you will attract the kind of partner who wants to be about the business of you. I don't believe the goal should be a healthy relationship. The healthy relationship is the foundation, there's so much more to be experienced with this person and I promise to never leave you or forsake you. Stay connected through all the various social media platforms, the website, the private community, seminars, retreats, and 1:1 group coaching opportunities that will be made exclusive only through the private community. We are a tribe because it takes a village. We are ever evolving beings and so are our relationships, but together, we are family. This is how we mix business with pleasure.

REFERENCES

Armagno, T. (2016). *Mark H. McCormack's What they don't teach you at Harvard Business School: Notes from a streetsmart executive - Summary.* Ant Hive Media.

Brown, J. (n.d.). The 7 million dollar habits. https://www.iamjoelbrown.com/the-7-million-dollar-habits/

Burkus, D. (2022, July 27). You are NOT the average of the five people you surround yourself with. Medium. https://medium.com/the-mission/youre-not-the-average of-the-five-people-you-surround-yourself-with-f21b817f6e69

Chronic illness & mental health. (2015). Bethesda, MD: National Institutes of Health, National Institute of Mental Health. 2015.

Clear, J. (n.d.). Successful people start before they feel ready. https://jamesclear.com/successful-people-start-before-they-feel-ready

Collins, J. C., & Lazier, W. C. (1995). *Beyond entrepreneurship: Turning your business into an enduring great company.* Prentice Hall.

Corley, T. C. (2016). The power of your network. https://richhabits.info/archives/8996

Diabetes and mental health. (2022). Centers for Disease Control. https://www.cdc.gov/diabetes/managing/mental-health.html

Eyal, N. (2021b, December 26). *You are Probably Thinking About Values All Wrong - Forge*. Medium. https://forge,-medium.com/you-don't-know-your-values-heres-why-thats-hurting-you-52b02a43e869

Forman, T. (2019) Self-care is not an indulgence. It is a discipline. https://pathforward.org/self-care-is-not-an-indulgence-its-a-discipline/?gclid=EAIaIQobCh-MI-Z2_-8LP-wIVHxXUAR3uhgw7EAAYAiAAEgIUtPD_BwE

Foster, S. (2021) *Survey: More than half of Americans couldn't cover three months of expenses with emergency savings.* https://www.bankrate.com/banking/savings/emergency-savings-survey-july-2021/ (Accessed: December 8, 2022).

GOBankingRates. (2022, August 25). 5 money questions to ask yourself to determine your financial health. https://www.gobankingrates.com/money/financial-planning/ask-yourself-questions-to-find-out-are-you-financially-healthy/

Kessler, R. C. et al. (2007). Lifetime prevalence and age-of-onset distributions of mental disorders in the World Health Organization's World Mental Health Survey Initiative. *World Psychiatry, 6*(3),168-176.

Key substance uses and mental health indicators in the United States: Results from the 2015 National Survey on

Drug Use and Health. (2016). Center for Behavioral Health Statistics and Quality. Substance Abuse and Mental Health Services Administration.

Kuska, A. M. (2019, August 26). *How a lifelong messy person can become neat.* https://www.myvetcandy.com/livingblog/2019/8/15/how-a-lifelong-messy-person-can-become-neat

Luchies, L. B., Wieselquist, J., Rusbult, C. E., Kumashiro, M., Eastwick, P. W., Coolsen, M. K., & Finkel, E. J. (2013). Trust and biased memory of transgressions in romantic relationships. *Journal of Personality and Social Psychology,104*(4), 673-694.

Markus, J. (n.d.). *What is branding?* https://www.oberlo.com/ecommerce-wiki/branding

Mental health: strengthening our response. (2022, June 17). https://www.who.int/news-room/fact-sheets/detail/mental-health-strengthening-our-response

Merikangas, K. R., He, J. P., Burstein, M., Swanson, S. A., Avenevoli, S., Cui, L., Benjet, C., Georgiades, K., & Swendsen, J. (2010). Lifetime prevalence of mental disorders in US adolescents: Results from the National Comorbidity Study-Adolescent Supplement (NCS-A). *Journal of the American Academy of Child and Adolescent Psychiatry, 49*(10), 980-989. doi: 10.1016/j.jaac.2010.05.017.

Psychology, P. (2022, December 9). *10 Habits of Great Relationships.* Practical Psychology. https://practicalpie.com/10-habits-of-great-relationships/

Sharpe, R. (2022, December 23). How to meet new people and find friends in 2023. https://declutterthemind.com/blog/how-to-meet-new-people/

Smith, A. T. (2022, March 27). 7 self-care tips for single moms. https://amyandrose.com/blogs/parenting/self-care-tips-for-single-moms/

Swartz, A. A. (2021, June 3). Abraham Hicks emotional guidance scale and how to use it. https://lifepurposeadvisor.com/abraham-hicks-emotional-guidance-scale-and-how-to-use-it/

www.ingramcontent.com/pod-product-compliance
Lightning Source LLC
LaVergne TN
LVHW051834080426
835512LV00018B/2876